For God and the Bible

FOR
GOD
AND THE
BIBLE

Jack L. Lease

VANTAGE PRESS
New York   Washington   Atlanta   Hollywood

Thanks and credit is given to the various authors and publishers who gave their permission to quote their works, as well as the many unnamed philosophers and thinkers who contributed ideas that went into the work, the whole, of course, being made possible by the Lord Jesus Christ in whom are hid all the treasures of wisdom and knowledge.

BT 102
.L4

SECOND PRINTING

Copyright © 1975 by Jack L. Lease

Published by Vantage Press, Inc.
516 West 34th Street, New York, New York 10001

Manufactured in the United States of America
Standard Book Number 533-02707-1

TO GOD

With thanks to the
Lord Jesus Christ

Contents

Introduction

Chapter One.   Starting Where You Are   1
    An invitation to a better life and an introduction to the
    Sophistical method of argumentation

Chapter Two.   God the Great Designer of the
                     Universe   8
    It contains elements of the teleological argument for
    God's existence—the argument from design—plus
    technical details concerning cosmology, with use of the
    work of Max Planck, Albert Einstein, and Fred Hoyle
    and Jayvant Narliker

Chapter Three.   God the Great Designer of Biological
                     Life   16
    It incorporates a mathematical analysis of design in
    biological life and logical argumentation regarding the
    interpretation of the evidence concerning mutations

Chapter Four.   God the Perfect Being   21
    It embodies the ontological argument for God's
    existence—the argument for God concerning
    being—with new analyses of the arguments and their
    implications

Chapter Five.   Being and the Lord Jesus Christ   27
    It embodies the substance of a paper written as a
    result of a discussion of the term "being" at a meeting
    of the Agoura, a monthly meeting of the faculty and
    majors in philosophy at the California State University

at Long Beach. It includes an analysis of the
implications of the miracles performed by Jesus Christ
and of the details surrounding His death and
resurrection

Chapter Six.   The Philosophy of the Golden Rule   30
    It embodies a religious and philosophical analysis of
    the Golden Rule given by Jesus Christ. The major part
    of the material was presented in a term paper for a
    class in American Philosophy taken at the California
    State University at Long Beach

Chapter Seven.   Biblical Criticism   40
    It embodies the material presented in a paper
    presented in a graduate school of religion class which
    analyzes the criticism of the Bible by the skeptical
    method and gives corresponding rebuttals as a
    Christian apology

Chapter Eight.   The Inspiration of the Scriptures   59
    It embodies material presented in a graduate school of
    religion class paper that analyzes skeptical criticism of
    Biblical inspiration and views influenced by the
    skeptical position to various degrees, and gives
    corresponding rebuttals from a fundamental point of
    view

Chapter Nine.   The Key Concept in the Thinking of
                the Apostle Paul   68
    A scholastic yet Biblical analysis of the chief concept in
    the thinking of the Apostle Paul with personal
    observations

Appendix.   The Role of Reason in Christian Ethics   75
    A religious yet technical analysis of the role of reason
    in Christian ethics. It includes part of the work of the
    philosopher Immanuel Kant which touches on
    elements related to the Sophistic method of
    argumentation (as well as valid argumentation)

Final Notes   81

Bibliography   85

Introduction

I trust that most everyone has had a difficult task. This book has the difficult task of reaching many kinds of people. One kind is the Christian whose faith is tried by a skeptical environment whose arguments are not so impressive when they are understood. This book endeavors to show that the skeptical criticism of God and the Bible is more than matched on a rational basis by logical arguments for God and the Bible so that the Bible is seen for what it is in truth, the Word of God.

Another kind of person is the rational but unsaved person whose mind is open to an honest argument for God and the Bible. He may have a desire for intellectual honesty but never realize that skeptical criticism of God and the Bible contains fallacies and has no real claim to intellectual honesty. This book can open up the way for this kind of person to come to God and the Bible by honestly considering what the Bible itself says.

Another kind is the person who has started on a downward path, who "couldn't care less" and is likely to reply "so what" to a scriptural admonition but can still be impressed by a consistent, logical argument. When this kind of person hits the bottom before they get the good news of the Gospel they often consider suicide. Many, especially college students, go all the way. This book is intended to reach them before they go all the way. If they can grasp the fact that criticism of God and the Bible contains fallacies they might grasp the idea that "It might be true after all and there is some hope."

Salvation is truly a matter of life and death, especially eternally. This is seen in the deathbed testimonies of atheists, many of which are recorded in a book. But before atheists reach the deathbed they are quite ready to reason to prove their views. Let us therefore reason together concerning God and the Bible.

My first wish is that, after the Bible, the reader could get hold of such books as *Science Speaks* by Dr. Peter Stoner, *Am I Intelligent?* by Raymond G. Hand, and *Count Down* by G. B. Hardy. These men have some really strong arguments for God. Philosophy has its usual arguments (cosmological—the argument for the existence of God from the necessity of assigning a cause or reason for the world; ontological—the argument that God's existence follows from His essence; teleological—the argument for God's existence taken from the evidences of order, design, contrivance, etc.) from which most of the arguments for God's existence derive, but when support is given from mathematics, biology, physics, and other sources, many interesting things are pointed out.

This book seeks to present some of the logical aspects of the *teleological argument*—the argument from design—as well as a revelation of what is behind fallacious Sophistical arguments that not only were used to counter various philosophical views but which have been used in arguing against all the arguments for God's existence. The Sophistical method seems to be at the root of many views that profess an indifferent or even negative view toward positive knowledge, morality, and even God. A clear understanding of how this method is related to Skepticism can help one to understand the present views of science and philosophy toward Nature, God, and the Bible.

Besides the consideration of views and methods of argument, an effort is made to point out to honest eyes the marks of God's handwork in Nature. Psalm19:1 says: "The heavens declare the glory of God and the earth showeth His handiwork." In the midst of Sophistical arguments which cause some to doubt but are often excused as mere tricks or jokes which are not to be taken seriously, I would like to point to real evidences and arguments for the existence of God. Playing tricks and making jokes with the Truth is serious as far as I am concerned. Man's happiness as well as his eternal destiny depends upon his relationship to God. If this book helps one person to see through some of the negative arguments that have tended to turn him away from a faith in the Living God, if this book helps one Christian to retain his faith in a skeptical environment, if this book saves one student (or nonstudent) from committing suicide, if this book helps one person come to the Lord Jesus Christ who can give eternal life, then it will have been worth all the effort that has gone into the making of it. The time may be very short for many to get the message.

For God and the Bible

Chapter One

Starting Where You Are

What do you want? A strengthening of faith? The good news that there is hope for the hopeless? The message about all these things is contained in the Bible. But many skeptical arguments have cast doubts about God and the Bible, so much so that even society is affected and a person can find himself in a "situational ethic" setting characterized by political questionings, economic uncertainty, and amorality with a continual weakening of public moral standards. The influence of all this upon a person's attempt to find real meaning in his life, happiness now, and a satisfying future is anything but helpful, to put it mildly.

However, a good look around will show that some people have found these things. These people are those who have not allowed doubts to prevent them from having faith in God and His Son Jesus Christ and the Bible. But in a world that is indifferent and sometimes critical of religion, especially in secular institutions of higher education, plenty of arguments have been put forth many of which are based on a clever but fallacious method of "reasoning" called Sophistry. Doubt the doubter, his motive and his method. René Descartes used doubt to find the indubital.

The Ancient Greek Sophists argued against the classicists and were shown to be in a worse position when Socrates

1

used their own method to reduce their position to a counter-dilemma. However, as the Classical school continued to perfect logic under Plato and Aristotle the Law of Noncontradiction was set forth. With the postulation of the Law of Noncontradiction the Sophistic method was shown to be clearly fallacious. But to people who are not familiar with the rules of logic, Sophistry could seem to be plausible although they have the feeling that something is wrong. In fact, the method was revived in the Middle Ages and used to criticize universals in logic and philosophy. Later, in the Renaissance, the method was used to criticize biblical doctrines, and finally, still later, the method was used to criticize the Bible itself.

With the revival of interest in science and the rise of the industrial society and the modern state, more interest was placed in material things while less interest was placed in spiritual things. The freedom to seek truth and to do good is also the freedom to use sophistries and to practice immorality. Deceit also began to play a large role in the modern world. Even in the world of literature not everyone realized the place that Sophistry played, but, of course, some did, for one of the seven types of art is Sophistication.

Let us therefore consider what Sophistry is and how it works. In general it is dramatic and seeks to build an image based upon appearances without real value behind it. In particular it uses propositions which are ambiguous and fallacious. Let us consider an example of ambiguity where it is not known which of two senses is meant:

> A Roman general once sent to the Oracle of Delphi to ask whether or not he would win in a battle with his enemy. The Oracle is reported to have replied: "The Romans can the enemy defeat."

Now the word "can" can be identified with "The Romans" or it can be identified with "the enemy." Thus two interpretations are possible: (1) "The Romans can" the enemy defeat; and (2) The Romans "can the enemy defeat." The position of the word "defeat" at the end of the sentence allows the ambiguous use of thé word "can."

Now consider the following syllogism:
Only material things are important.
Religion is immaterial.
Therefore religion is unimportant.

The word "immaterial" in the minor premise (second sentence) is used in two senses. One, in relation to "material" in the major premise (first sentence) as something "nonmaterial," that is, "nonphysical." Two, in relation to "unimportant" in the conclusion (last sentence) as something "nonimportant."

The ancient Greek philosopher Zeno of Elea devised many paradoxes. An apparently previous argument among philosophers concerning the bisecting of a geometrically constructed line held, on the one side, that the two end points defining a line would lose their magnitude and finite dimensions if the line were infinitely divided. Thus it was concluded that a line is composed of an infinite number of points each of which has location but no physical magnitude, has position but no finite dimensions (existing as an idea in the realm of thought, or abstract space). The other side held that a line is the shortest distance between two points each of which is the smallest point discernible to the senses. The points and the line drawn between them are the finest and smallest that can be mechanically constructed by man and discerned by his senses.

One of his paradoxes was designed to show that motion is impossible. It goes like this: Achilles shoots an arrow at a rabbit, but before it can go all the way it must go one-half the way. And before it can go the remaining half, it must go one-half of that. Now the arrow is at rest at each point in its traverse since each point has location but no finite magnitude and since all the points of rest cannot add up to motion, motion is impossible. Note that the "idea" of motion to a point ($\frac{1}{2}$, $\frac{1}{4}$, $\frac{1}{8}$) which has position but no physical dimensions or magnitude is set against the "process" of motion. The word "motion" is used in two senses, moving to a point and moving in traverse.

As was mentioned above, during the Middle Ages, after the Greek period, universals were attacked. Still later in the Renaissance, when the rational aspect of philosophical consideration became one school (Rationalism) and the physical aspect became another (Empiricism), Sophism developed into Skepticism. At this point let the reader remember that when Socrates used the Sophistic method against the Sophists themselves they were reduced to a worse counterdilemma than Socrates had been.

Sophism depends upon fallacy and valid logic depends upon the Law of Noncontradiction in a large measure. The Skeptics have denied that there are any universals. They therefore have to reject the Law of Noncontradiction as a universal statement. When this is done contradiction is directly or indirectly allowed and this is a part of the Sophistic method. Therefore there is a relationship between the Sophistic method and the Skeptical method. Therefore let us consider the "reasoning" of the Skeptics.

When we examine the "pattern" of Skeptical arguments we find this form according to A. J. Ayer: (1) Skepticism asserts that we depend entirely upon the premises for our knowledge of the conclusion; (2) that the relation between the premises and the conclusion is *not* deductive; (3) that the relation between the premises and the conclusion is *not* inductive; and (4) that since the inferences can be justified neither deductively nor inductively, they cannot be . . . justified at all (1, in Bibliography).

Now the skeptics who made these assertions also said that because there are no absolutes or true universals, no major premise in a syllogism can be "distributed" (a distributed premise applies and holds true 100% throughout the universe of discourse in which it is involved) or universal. Therefore deductions made by a syllogism are not valid. They also said that since there are no absolutes or universals and since all the evidence is not in, and that it must always be

4

possible to introduce new evidence (and the implication would seem to be that all the evidence can never be in) therefore no inference is truly valid (or "doesn't apply to real life"). It appears that they should have used the word "valid" in the sense of allowing the possibility of deduction and induction but they flatly said that the nature of the relation between the premises and the conclusion was not "deductive" nor was it "inductive."

If this liberty was taken in the opposite direction a charge of committing the fallacy of "each to all" (one is, so all are) could be lodged thusly: When you say that the relation between the premises and the conclusion is not deductive because there are no absolutes or universals to be used in the major premise (and sometimes in the minor premise) you are reasoning in this manner: "There is one case where the major premise is not universal (or minor premise is not universal), therefore *all* cases are cases where the major premise (or minor premise) is not universal." And likewise with "induction"; "There is one case where the evidence is not all in and the major (or minor) premise is not universal and the relation between the premises and the conclusion is not inductive. Therefore all cases are cases where that is true."

But without going this far it is sufficient to point out that the denial of universals and absolutes is circular: How do you know that there are *no* absolutes or universals, because according to you there are no deductive or inductive processes of reasoning by which you can arrive at that absolute, universal conclusion? It is also possible to point to the commission of "The Fallacy of Two Negatives" (from two negative premises, no valid conclusion may be reached). One negative is: "The relation between the premises and the conclusion is *not* deductive." The other negative is: "The relation between the premises and the conclusion is *not* inductive."

It is laborious for the reader to follow this exposition of reasoning if he has not had logic, but it can be rewarding for him if he wishes to understand the nature of fallacious and valid reasoning that has not only in a great measure shaped his society and educational world but in particular application has been applied to things from simple logic on up to the philosophy of science, and from law to theology.

This controversy over the possibility of absolutes and universals caused many scientists to hold theories "tentatively" and to seek a "unity of science" related to a "unity of language." The relation of language to science and philosophy, as regards interpretation and description is shown by John G. Kemeny in his book, *A Philosopher Looks At Science*. He says in it: "Suppose the scientist has some entities he wants to study, together with certain relations holding between them. He will then search for a branch of mathematics whose system of axioms, *when interpreted*, will correctly describe the entities and the relations he wants to study" (27 in Bibliography).

Some interpretations seem to be honest and to search for the truth. Some seem to be otherwise. Consider how much interpretation and description enter into science and philosophy, especially if a person has a particular impression he wishes to create or a doctrine he wishes to support. A. J. Ayer, again, says:

> This is not to say that philosophers are not concerned with facts, but they are in the strange position that all the evidence which bears upon their problems is already available to them. It is not further scientific information that is needed to decide such philosophical questions as whether the material world is real, whether objects continue to exist at times when they are not perceived, whether other human beings are conscious in the same sense as one is oneself. These are not questions that can be settled by experiment, since the way in which they are answered itself determines how the result of any experiment is to be interpreted. What is in dispute in such cases is not whether, in a given set of circumstances, this or that event will happen, but rather how anything at all that happens is to be described. (1, p. 2 in Bibliography).

Therefore if God and the Bible are described in terms of conscious Sophistry and Skepticism the impression will be one of doubt and unbelief. Sometimes the goal of such description is to create an attitude of indifference and unconcern. If the Sophistical and Skeptical methods of argument are understood a person is ready to consider descriptions of God and the Bible in terms of faith and credibility.

Chapter Two

God the Great Designer of the Universe

It was once boasted that "Matter always was. It can be neither created nor destroyed." This position was adopted when some men held that the indivisible building blocks of the universe were atoms. Some men, aware of course, of heat, light, electricity and magnetism contemplated the universe as "a mere quantity of energy." Albert Einstein was a brilliant mathematician and theoretical physicist. He believed in God but did not believe that He was a personal God. He postulated the Law of the Conversion of Mass and Energy, $E = MC^2$ (in the conversion of mass into energy the amount of energy is equal to the amount of mass multiplied by the square of a constant, the speed of light) after considering Max Planck's quantum theory of the definite energy of radiations (in any radiation the energy emitted mathematically divided by the frequency of the radiation equals a constant—Planck's constant "h"—and is expressed by the formula $E = hV$. The frequency is inversely proportional to the velocity, $1/F = V$, and $E/F = h$ is the same as $E = hV$. Dividing by the frequency, F, on the left hand side of the equation is equal to multiplying by the velocity, V, on the right hand side). (2, in Bibliography.)

If a person follows Einstein's thinking from the point of view of mathematics and theoretical physics he can see a quantification of the universe, first under the Theory of Special Relativity (time and space are one and are relative) and then under the Unified Field Theory (gravity and magnetism are manifestations of a single, more fundamental entity). Mathematical quantification of forces and electrical fields suggested to him that space is bent in or "warped" in places. A person can conceive of the universe generally as a sphere not too different, perhaps, from a large glass sphere with stars in it. Under Einstein's view this sphere won't be a perfect sphere but would be bent in, in places. Some suggested that the form of the universe is like a saddle. There seems to be reasons that suggest to some that the universe has the form of a doughnut. These "forms" are conceived because the universe is quantified and then geometricized as in the case of the geometry of the Unified Field Theory. Thus some conceive of mathematical models of the universe. The form, order, and design of the universe, seen from these considerations, show the presence of the Great Designer of the universe, God.

But a critic, setting the rational aspect of the universe against the empirical aspect could say: "Light travels at a constant speed (approximately 186, 284 miles per second), and calculations involving this figure show the universe to be so great in magnitude (a great distance for light to travel) and duration (a long time for light to travel) that the biblical statement about the universe being created in four days, Genesis 1:3-19, cannot be true and therefore the Bible is false and there is no God."

In answer to this it may be said: "Either God is almighty or He is not God at all." He is not limited to the things He created, including light and the speed at which He ordained that it should travel. When man theorizes about the age of the universe, he postulates (that is, some men do) that age as at an extreme of about 9.6 billion years. But take a figure a little greater, ten billion years. This number may be represented in exponential or mathematical "power" form as ten to the ninth power, 10^9. But God is infinite. If 10^9 is divided by infinity the number approaches zero. Mathematically this would be up to but not including zero (the mathematical prescription is "divide by x as x approaches infinity). Thus considered, it is seen to approach the limit zero. It is a creature of God, a creation. Here is the point—the agnostics or skeptical critics could say: "The universe is 9.6 billion years old and there cannot be a God." They are comparing physics with metaphysics (realm of thought and spirit). The reply compares mataphysics with physics using infinity to infer a metaphysical reduction of the opposite import.

In like manner men, by the use of mathematics and electromagnetic impulses received by electronic telescopes, calculated the farthest star known or suspected, to be possibly eight billion light-years away from the earth. If the earth is taken as the center of the universe, the distance across the universe, two radii of eight billion light-years each, is sixteen billion light-years (a light-year is the distance that light can travel in one year). This may be represented exponentially (as a "power") as 1.6^{10}, that is, 1.6 to the tenth power. Now again, if this figure is divided by infinity the quotient, that is, the resulting figure would approach zero. Thus considered it is seen to approach a limit. It is a creature, a creation of God. The argumentive import is the same as for the consideration of time.

Again, the critic could say in reply: "The most you can do is to equate God with infinity, which does not necessarily follow." When the assertion is made that: "It is a creature, a creation of God," again a critic could say: "Time is a product of the motion of the planets. The postulation of the eternality of matter is just as valid as the postulation of biblical creation and time, as the product of the motion of eternal matter is eternal. And if eternal time is divided by infinity its magnitude does not approach zero and it is thus a natural entity. Thus no Creator is needed to explain it." But this does not take into account the latest theories concerning the expansion of the universe. The mathematical calculation of the inverse or reverse of the expansion of the universe points to a primary mass of material at a definite time. But an agent caused it to explode, if the expansion theory is accepted. This is seen by considering the sun and reasoning backwards. The sun is fusioning. It had to start or be started fusioning. Otherwise it would be a planet. But there are millions of suns (stars). If the statement is postulated that they were all blown out into space when the "primary mass" exploded (or was exploded), there still remains to be explained why some of the primary mass became suns and some planets. Rather, a "selective" than a general process is seen, and this implies an agent. The implications of the 'selective process' include the causing of the explosion of the primary mass, the causing of some of the material blown outward to be planets and some to be "suns" (stars) and the starting of the fusioning of the sun, among other things. And on this basis the agent is the Creator of time.

So likewise can the critic reason for distance, saying that the universe "may" be infinite in dimensions and infinite space divided by infinity does not approach zero and it is thus a natural entity needing no Creator to explain it. Originally it was stated only that the quotient "approached zero." There still remains a division between the finite, which is the realm of material things, and the infinite, which is the realm of spiritual things. However, the critic is "reasoning" only from an uncertain "may." The two turning points are: "God is infinite" and "The universe may be infinite in dimensions." But again the mathematical calculation of the reverse of the expansion process of the universe points to a primary mass and an "agent." The agent inhabits the realm of the infinite but material things the realm of the finite.

The skeptic who denies universals and yet seeks to prove that there is no evidence of God the Great Designer in the universe not only has no claim on logic but contradicts himself, making, himself, a universal statement. But even in terms of mathematics the skeptic is worsted, for one late theory in cosmology given by Fred Hoyle and his mathematician friend, Jayvant V. Narliker, the theory of continuous creation, holds that "The universe is still being formed out of nothing in empty space" (*Time Magazine*, Science Section, July 3, 1964) (22 in Bibliography).

Hoyle and Narliker's theory, purported to be supported by mathematics, claims to explain why galaxies in distant parts of the universe can, theoretically, move away from the earth "faster than the speed of light . . . a speed that Einstein said could not be exceeded."

Now it is also possible to show that the speed of light can be exceeded by referring to the phenomenon in science known as the "red shift." When light comes from a source moving away from the earth at high speeds the frequency of the light is normal, but because of the greater distance it has to cover its net frequency is lower, putting it in the range of the lower part of the visible spectrum next to the infrared band. The "shift" in net frequency toward the lower "red" end of the visible spectrum is proportional to the speed at which the light-emitting body is moving away from the observer. So when it is determined by a "red shift" that a body is moving away from the earth at 90 percent of the speed of light, it is logical to suppose that if a similar body is moving away from the earth at exactly the same speed in exactly the opposite direction the speed at which the two bodies are moving away from each other is 90 percent plus 90 percent or 180 percent of the speed of light.

Now if the observer were on one of the two bodies which were moving away from each other at 180 percent of the speed of light, he would never see the light from the other body. It would be invisible as far as he was concerned. These are put forth to show that if the speed of light can be exceeded, why limit God to the speed of light and say that the universe could not be created in four days? God said "Let there be light" (Gen. 1:3), and this does not mean that it took billions of years to happen. God's almighty power is the answer.

And when it is seen that under certain conditions (noted above) light from a light-emitting body can be invisible, who can exhaustively limit and define the things that are invisible (besides the invisible portions of the electromagnetic spectrum)? Now some criticize the idea that God created the universe *ex nihilo* (out of nothing). As a step in the right direction a critic should admit the possibility that God created the visible things from the invisible things. Later, prehaps, he can go all the way to the truth: "For by Him were all things created, that are in heaven and that are in earth, visible and invisible" (Col. 1:16a). Again God's almighty power is the answer.

Work involving the transformation of subatomic particles in high-energy accelerators and cyclotrons into matter has shown a "complimentarity" of such a nature that there is a "rush of nature," so to speak, to fill in the vacuum or partial vacuum near the particles to complete the structure. It has already been noted in Max Planck's formula $E = hV$ and in Albert Einstein's $E = MC^2$ that the Great Designer, God, uses precise order and contrivance in His work. But with respect to the various theories of men concerning the creation of the universe, the inferences may be put: If it be stated that the universe is a mere quantity of energy, then the order, complimentarity, and contrivance apparent in the universe must be accounted for. If it be stated that energy and matter always existed in interaction, the elements of order, complimentarity and contrivance must be accounted for in addition to the fact that the universe is apparently expanding. The scientific consideration is based on the inference "if-then"; if the outer parts of the universe are expanding then one infers that the expansion started at one point. The author believes all the parts of the universe were created in their positions of a few thousand years ago and set in the motions they now have. It is simply a matter of power. The details of creation imply processes that take time, but the total inference of all facts and processes imply an Almighty Creator that set the processes in motion. He did and does have the power to contrive a set of conditions in process or motion with the appearances as if they were in process of long continuance. God is not limited by any aspect of the Creation He created. The "stage" of Creation was "set" for man's sake, created in God's image, to declare God's glory and show his handiwork (Psalm 19:1). This "purpose" is a factor in the consideration. (Also, one radiocarbon test indicates that the age of the earth is 14,000 years.) At what point and when did it begin to expand and why? The Bible has the answers, but man cannot come to them until he first relinquishes doubt and has faith. Even Christians "know in part" (20 I Cor. 13:9) but believe for the rest.

If a critic doubts and holds that "matter always was; It can be neither created nor destroyed," let him also consider that "God always was; He can be neither created nor destroyed." The real victory comes to one who has faith. The Scripture says: "Through faith we understand that the worlds were framed by the Word of God, so that things which are seen were not made by things which do appear" (20, Heb. 11:3). The critic might say: "I would like to believe that but I need help." In answer it may be said—Honestly consider the indications of the handiwork of God in nature. Look at the snowflake. Each snowflake has a definite, unique, geometrical design and no two snowflakes are exactly alike. Only an all-intelligent Great Designer could have made them. The earth is tilted at just the right angle (23.5 degrees) from a perpendicular axis in its orbit around the sun to give proper seasons. The earth is just the right distance from the sun. If it were a little farther away from the sun the polar ice caps would increase and the earth would be frozen. If it were a little closer to the sun the polar ice caps would melt, the ocean level would rise, and much land would be covered with water and the atmosphere would be unbearably hot and humid. The atmosphere of the earth contains the proper amounts of oxygen and nitrogen to support life (except for pollution). There is no other known place in the universe where the same set of conditions exist. Even the sun and the moon have no apparent purpose except to provide warmth and light for man on earth and with the stars to provide times and seasons and plant growth. The Scripture says: "For the invisible things of Him from the creation of the world are clearly seen, being understood by the

and the RNA of the genes of the cell, we have the statement that they are "genetic codes" made up of four basic "building blocks." Since chemical laws are limited, and choice, design, and purpose are evident in the assembling of these "building blocks" in various intelligent combinations in the genetic code, it is evident that a Designing Mind is present. Dr. Pollard in his book *Chance and Providence* reports a factor of ten to the sixty-fourth power against evolution. Dr. J. T. Jukes (page 227, June, 1963, *American Scientist*) points out that: "There can exist about four times seventy to the eighty-seventh power nucleic acids." These figures were arrived at in DNA (genetic code) studies. Even if a cell progression "evolved" one genetic change in the genetic code per second it would pass the ten to the seventeenth power seconds figure given by some as the lifetime of the earth, before it began to approach the 4×70 to the eighty-seventh power figure for possible nucleic acids (15, p. 5).

When one tries to show that mutations can be caused by the introduction of chemicals into cells and cell environment and that growth is therefore according to chemical and other laws only, it should be remembered that three things are involved: (1) the chemical introduced; (2) the mind that introduced the chemical; and (3), the fact that the introduction of the chemical is artificial and is not likely to occur in nature.

When animals lose limbs and even heads, and these are replaced, the replacement of that which was lost goes beyond natural chemical and physical laws. To disprove this by the contradiction of this, that "replacement is according to natural and chemical laws only", one must show that a "replay" of the "genetic code" is not by a mind that "decides" where to start the "tape" and where to stop it. How can chemical parts "decide" these things?

In going to the "issue" of biology, that of the genetic code, we passed by the question of "What is Life?" Science, without explaining life, has defined characteristics of life such as the ability to move toward food, to move away from danger, to reproduce, and others. The ordinary cell "takes in"

17

food material through its cell membrane and "sends out" waste materials, but an ameba is a single-celled organism capable of locomotion so that the characteristics just immediately mentioned before actually apply from a single cell on up. A crystal can grow by the chemical addition of atoms, but there is no genetic code in crystal structure and no "sending out" of materials. Between this and the ameba there is the Mosaic Tobacco Virus. When it is hydrated, that is, contains water, it's considered as living. When it is dehydrated it is considered a chemical. If the skeptical critic says 'The water gives it life and it is a natural process which requires no supernatural agent' he is violating J. S. Mills's scientific cannon of the 'method of differences'; if water is added to ten chemicals one of which is the Mosaic Tobacco Virus and it only is considered as living, the difference and hence the 'cause' of being considered as living is not the water but something else, for they all had water added unto them. The believer could say: 'The spirit of life uses the water: but the believer could also recognize that the virus was formed as a result of the curse put upon nature when Adam fell in the Garden of Eden (20, Genesis 3:17). A simple reply of a believer could be 'God both made the water and gives life.' A curse is involved (20, Genesis 3:17, 18).

When an organism moves there is a coordinated harmony among the parts of the organism initiated by an "impulse." This impulse is beyond electrostatic discharge, chemical attraction or heat production only. When fish eggs are buried in the sand they remain inert until they are reached by the highest wave at a certain period. When the salt water hits them they immediately hatch. One could say that the eggs respond to water and sodium chloride, a chemical-only response. A reply to this is that a Mind guided the mother fish to place her eggs at "just the right" distance up the beach so that she could get back into the sea (she chose "just the right wave" to come in on) and also that the eggs would *not* be reached by another wave until an incubation period had elapsed. A "Mind" determined that the eggs should not only respond to the sea

18

water as a hatching agent but also as a "signal" to the newly hatched fish that the "means" of escape from the sand to the sea had arrived. The response was no less a "life" response than a chemical one. A critic would say: "I reject the idea that 'The Spirit of Life uses water' with respect to the Mosaic Tobacco Virus and the 'life-response' with respect to the fish." In response a reply may be made to the critic: "Well, what are you going to do with this. A number of people were wrecking a building. When they got to the cornerstone of the building, which was made of concrete, and which had the date of its pouring for the dedication of the building thirty years previously, they began to break it in two with an air hammer. When they split it out jumped a frog that had obviously been entombed for thirty years.

If we attempt to define "life" on a rational basis we could give an insufficient but "fair" definition as "the directed ability to manifest the characteristics ascribed to life." A real explanation and definition is given in the Bible which is no less a source of information than the Book of Nature. Should not someone who wants "all the evidence in" at least consider what the Bible says? The New Testament says in John 1:1-4: "In the beginning was the Word, and the Word was with God and the Word was God. All things were made by Him and without Him was nothing made that was made. In Him was Life and the Life was the Light of men." How else could a little bird get both the "ability" and the "direction" to fly 7,000 miles across land and sea to land on a small island if this were not true?

Without arguing this further, when we come to man we find an organism that can deal with its environment when it is symbolically represented to it. We find an organism that can design, purpose, and invent, thus showing mind and its origin and relationship to a Mind-Giver. This shows that mind is given, made present to and sustained for one by a Mind-Giver. Psalm 22:29 in the Bible says: "And none can keep alive his own soul." Arguments against these contentions may be made but they do not meet the test of truth,

19

consistencey. More consistency is to be found in postulating that there is a designing, mind-giving Mind to be found in biological life than not.

Chapter Four

God the Perfect Being

Anselm, a medieval Christian philosopher, reflected upon existence and being. He noted human qualities in their limited form and noted degrees leading in the direction of perfection. The conception of being in humans leads up to, but not including, perfect being. But the human mind can conceive of being outside and beyond itself, Perfect Being. Man is finite but he can conceive of the ideas of the infinite. He is intelligent, has some power, some handsomeness and beauty. But he can conceive of these qualities in their perfect form. God has Perfect Being and is Perfect Being and has all these qualities perfectly.

Critics have stated that if one begins by "defining" God as existing, then one is "begging the question," that is, assuming what is to be proved. Modern logic does not accept universals, per se, as true in themselves. It requires propositions to be existentially qualified, asking for If God exists, then so and so. It also uses propositions once they are *assumed*. Therefore, if logic is to be allowed in the consideration, proposions must be used which are taken by faith, assumed or existentially qualified. But regardless of how the propositions are qualified the essential character of logic remains, that is, systematicity, and an appeal to logic is an appeal to systematic thinking.

If the critic therefore is willing to think logically then let us first begin with man for the critic's sake seeing that God does not criticize Himself as not existing.

Men have conceived of different systems of thought. They have built different systems on different points of view, different feelings, different affinities. Systems have been built upon "being," "flux and change," "deceit" (sophistry), "abstraction" (idealism), "balance" (immanent idealism and the Golden Mean), "pleasure" (Epicureanism), "doubt" (skepticism), "common sense" (ecclecticism), "mystery" (Pythagoreanism), "wholeness" (monism), "deeds" (pragmatism), "human senses" (Empiricism), "feeling" (emotionalism,) "impulse" (vitalism) and "intuition." However, all these basically reduce to seven types: naturalism, pragmatism, dualism, realism, intuition, mysticism, and idealism.

"Naturalism considers the whole of reality to be in nature, regarding Nature as the sum total of objects in space, time, and sense subject to causal natural laws. Therefore, only nature exists and from it mind and reason emerge." "Pragmatism appeals to the will to achieve conclusions, distrusts *pure reason* AND intellect. It is a form of action regarding ideas, beliefs, etc. as tools in the business of living." "Dualism is the recognition of two irreducible principles, such as body and mind." "Realism generally recognizes the independent reality of the experienced world." "Intuition is direct or immediate knowing without known cognition." "Mysticism is immediate experience of reality through a special mode of knowing independent of perceptions" "Idealism as a whole is conceived in terms or ideas interpreted in various ways" (3, pp. 146-250 in Bibliography).

Now all of these have this in common: They are human and they are systematic. Now any system has certain characteristics. It has a fundamental point of view, a generic assumption, a point of initial and important reference or some essential consideration. Around this are usually instituted some secondary considerations. These must be related to the primary consideration and derive their meaning from it and in terms of it. The secondary considerations must be consistent with one another and with the primary consideration simultaneously. Further considerations must all be related to the primary and secondary considerations. The primary consideration is applied to the secondary and tertiary (third) considerations, and they respectively refer to the primary consideration. All interpretation of everything else is based upon these. (In geometry the system includes self-evident assumptions, axioms, postulates, and theorems.) But these aforementioned seven systems are limited. This is seen in the fact that they do not relate to each other to make a systematic whole. They are considered by one who studies philosophy and are related to human nature, but they are like human thought in general; it leads in the direction of perfection. It leads up to but not including perfection.

Now the point in all these considerations so far is the same: The conception of limitedness in a human frame of reference and the conception of perfection outside and beyond the human frame of reference. The conception in man points to the reality beyond him.

When we look at the seven philosophical systems, for instance, we notice that something is lacking to make them act together as a whole in harmony, in light, and in unity. It is true that each one has advantages and makes contributions, but the arguments and the discord among them hinders the great contributions they could all make acting as a concerted whole. There is a *sine qua non*, an essential condition without which the goal cannot be accomplished. The problem is similar to that which any system would have if it did not have a primary principle or point of reference which is applied to the whole system and to which the elements of the system relate for operation, meaning and validity. (That primary principle is the will of God. Now "will" may be viewed as foreign to the sense of the whole argument and consideration. But please notice that the relevancy is this; the elements of the philosophical systems have their existence in human being but could have their perfection in the Divine Being.) These aforementioned assertions point in the direction of the conclusion of the argument. They need only the establishment of the logical connection between man and God with respect to the idea in man and the reality in God.

One attempt to reach the conclusion apart from the consideration of man endeavors to "prove" the existence of God by appealing to the logical consideration of being classified into categories. In terms of possibilities being may be characterized first as "being" and "nonbeing" and subcategorized as "possible," "contingent," and "necessary" being. In trying to place God in one of these categories one may say that the idea of God is not impossible in that it is not "self-contradictory." And if one is to deal with the idea of God at all one cannot categorize Him as "unnecessary being." Thus one cannot place God in the category of "impossible, unnecessary being." The next category is contingent being. First, negatively, perhaps God does not exist but He may come into being. But this is insufficient, for God must have always existed if He be true God and one coming into existence cannot be God. Thus God cannot be placed in the category of negative, insufficient, contingent being. Then, positively, perhaps God does exist but He may cease to exist. This is sufficient for human being (viewed physically) but not for divine being. If God be true God, He cannot cease to exist. He thus cannot be placed in the category of positive, sufficient, contingent being. He must be placed in the category of Necessary Being. Finally, if a being is necessary, it exists.

A critic might say: "While it is admitted God might exist, the category of 'necessary' is set in a contrived diagram." But the reply is that, as was shown before, the argument reverts to a human frame of reference in general and to man's ability to conceive in particular. Starting with the undeniable fact of man's existence it is necessary to admit that the man who conceived of the diagram conceived of the category of necessity. Now since man is not a necessary being the idea of a necessary being must have its source beyond man. Therefore just as the idea of Perfect Being is beyond man and the idea of necessary being is beyond man and every transcendental is beyond man (including eternity and infinity), they can have their source only in a Perfect Being. Man therefore can conceive of his being and the Perfect Being. The idea of perfection can exist in man but perfection itself can exist only in "the" Perfect Being. Man cannot conceive of a being greater than Perfect Being. Again, if a critic denies this and starts a series thus: "He is 'a' perfect being, this other man is 'a' more perfect being, and this third man is 'a' still more perfect being, thus taking steps of 'still more,' 'still more'," and so on, the critic is only contributing to the ultimate definition of God as "that being greater than which it is not possible to conceive" (The critic uses "a" before "perfect being.")

W. T. Jones makes a comment on this which is relevant:

> It is clear, then, that a being that does not exist cannot be most perfect and, conversely, that the most perfect being must exist. In other words, the "than-which-nothing-is-greater" being would not be the "than-which-nothing-is-greater" if it did not exist.

> It is evident that Anselm's proof is open to attack at two main points: (1) Do we in fact have an idea of an absolutely perfect being? (2) Is existence an "added perfection"? Is a being that exists greater (more perfect) than one that does not exist? Both these points were raised almost immediately by the monk named Gaunilo, and they have continued to be discussed by philosophers and theologians from that day to this. (25, pp. 434, 435 in Bibliography)

In answer to these questions the author would say yes. Observable degrees of perfection in humans give rise to the aforementioned line of reasoning, and we do indeed have an idea of an absolutely Perfectly Being. Also why should anyone be concerned with a being that does not exist?

The cause must be greater than the effect or equal to it.

Man has the concept of Perfect Being but does not have Perfect Being itself. Therefore the cause of the concept of Perfect Being cannot be merely equal to the effect. It must therefore be greater than the effect. Now since the concept of Perfect Being in man must have its origin in Perfect Being itself and since Perfect Being is the cause and is greater than the concept of Perfect Being in man, therefore both in terms of concept and cause, Perfect Being exists.

Therefore we do not simply define God as existing. We prove Perfect Being, and define God as Perfect Being. (While this is logical one cannot help but be grateful for God's revelation that tells us that the pure in heart shall see God.)

Chapter Five

Being and the Lord Jesus Christ

In a meeting of the Agoura, a monthly meeting of the faculty and majors in philosophy at the California State University, at Long Beach, the moderator asked the question: "What shall we do with the term being?" After various comments I quoted John 1:1-9. At the end of the discussion I said: "I believe in the Bible for my eternal salvation but let me say this: A mind in the light is something but a mind in the dark is nothing." I didn't give any explanation, but what I meant was that souls who die without Christ the Light live on in the nothingness of darkness and death. They exist as a soul or mind but do have being as could be said of Abel: "He being dead yet speaketh," (Heb. 4:11), or of Abraham, Isaac, and Jacob: "Wherefore He is not the God of the dead, but of the living." (20, Luke 20: 38)

But in looking at the question in John 1:1-9, we see three categories given in, by, and through the Lord Jesus Christ: light, life, and things. Philosophy debates the pros and cons of the existence of God and while some philosophers believe in God and others do not, the arguments either way are not unquestioned. In the realm of philosophy, therefore, it may be said you can neither prove nor disprove the existence of God to the satisfaction of all, even though those denying are without excuse according to Romans 1:20.

Plants and animals, marvels of "moving matter," show God's handiwork, but science cannot answer the question: "What is life and where did it come from?" Man is a still greater marvel of "moving matter" possessing reason and an immortal soul. The fact that man can lose both shows his divine, not natural, origin. Philosophy has yet to answer the question of exactly how the human mind can be aware of its own thoughts and reflections. Although the elements of mind, thought, and reflection be present, the "how" of awareness above the animal level cannot be answered apart from God because the "how" of mental illumination cannot be answered apart from God. To describe the fact and effect of mental light, be it called reason or any other name, does not explain, apart from God, the communication of all this with the personality "I." René Descartes did not write: "Think, therefore am" but "I think, therefore I am." There is thinking, God for example, "My thoughts are not your thoughts (Old Testament Scripture) and being, angels for example, apart from the personality "I", but they are known when they are communicated. Mentally ill persons are often considered as legally nonexistent. They do not perform, universally, acts showing the use of the light. Does not this all indicate that awareness is "brought" to mind when mind has awareness at all above the animal level (of course the normal mind is an "inquiring mind" at times) ? Is not the confrontation of a mind with writing in a foreign language a test? The awareness of marks is given but not the awareness of thoughts except the thoughts be brought to the mind by a mind previously knowing them. The nearest philosophy can come to explaining the "how" is to postulate ideas, categories, blank tablets, closets, and flowings of consciousness which bear witness of the light and its work without stating that the light brings things *to* personalities. (One philosopher held that the mind is a bundle of perceptions and so it is, in a sense, when one is estranged from God.)

But we need not have any doubt since God fully revealed Himself in His Son, the Lord Jesus Christ. Jesus said: "But the

Comforter, which is the Holy Ghost, whom the Father will send in My name, he shall teach you all things, and bring all things to your remembrance, whatsoever I have said unto you" (20, John 14:26).

Jesus demonstrated "being" in His power in "extended" time in fulfilling prophecies; in "contracted" time in working miracles of bread, wine, fishes, and healings; over matter in walking on the water and in being transformed on the Mount of Transfiguration. He demonstrated that "In Him all things consist" (20, Col. 1:17), that He upholds all things by the word of His power (20, Heb. 1:3), at least by odds of four to one (if it be not taken in faith) when He died upon the cross, because four things happened simultaneously: He cried out, His heart rent, the veil of the temple rent, and the earth, rocks, and graves rent in an earthquake. He demonstrated "being," however, beyond all odds when He rose from the grave. Who can deny these demonstrations of "being" by the Lord Jesus Christ?

Thus it is written that "your faith should stand, not in the wisdom of men but in the power of God" (20, I Cor. 2:5). What is the power of God? "For I am not ashamed of the gospel of Christ, for it is the power of God unto salvation to everyone that believeth" (20, Rom. 1:16).

Chapter Six

The Philosophy of the Golden Rule

This chapter is mainly the body of a paper presented in a class on American philosophy at a state university. Therefore it is the product of an effort to present a religious theme in a class in philosophy whose emphasis was mainly empirical and pragmatic. Certain terms are used with which the reader may be unfamiliar. "A Priori" refers to that which is "before experience" such as an idea, a form, or something from the realm of thought, things of a rational or mental nature. For instance, an "A Priori" judgment is one in which a universal and necessary connection of the subject with the predicate is made. A "Synthetic" judgment is one in which the predicate is not contained in the subject. (See "The Role Of Reason In Christian Ethics" in Appendix.) "Metaphysics" deals with concern for the ultimate nature of things.

The Old Testament says in the Book of Proverbs, Chapter Nine, verse ten: "The fear of the Lord is the beginning of wisdom: and the knowledge of the holy is understanding." In *Euthyphro*, by Plato, Socrates carries on a discussion with Euthyphro concerning piety or holiness. The Greeks may have gotten some of their wisdom from King Solomon, for people from all over the world came to see the Temple and to hear him. At any rate God is the giver of wisdom.

In *The Republic*, Plato builds on the main theme of the

book, the Rule Of Life (justice, temperance, courage, and wisdom). Aristotle builds upon the rule of life embodied in the Golden Mean and imminent idealism (form in substance).

When the Lord Jesus Christ came to earth, He said: "But, behold, a greater than Solomon is here." He gave us the Golden Rule. This Rule, in its statement and practice, comprises the greatest philosophy ever given to man. Please consider a view of it in some of its aspects.

The Golden Rule as given by the Lord Jesus Christ in the Sermon on the Mount in the New Testament, the Book of Matthew, chapters five to seven: "Therefore, all things whatsoever ye would that men should do to you, do ye even so to them: for this is the law and the prophets."

The world as naturally constituted is self-interested. In the abstract structure of self-interest thinking, dependence holds the central place. In the concrete structure of self-interest acting power holds the central place. Thus, the "a priori" of dependence joins with the "synthetic" of power to form the "synthetic-a priori," so to speak, of self-interest existence. (This only means that human nature in itself desires independence from and power over everything. Actually, of course, these are obtained in various degrees.) Thus from this solipistic (selfish) center relations with God, man, and nature are characterized by independence from and power over, them, while they are reduced to dependence and powerlessness. (That is not the case but would be if the relation were completely established.) This key is seen as a factor in the rise and fall of nations (although the will of God is being done) and in the dialectic of doctrines from the earliest times down to the present. Even science and philosophy can be explained, in part, in positive, negative, and mixed forms of this key.

But all this is self-defeating in a large measure because the trinity of self, independence, and power constitutes a world that is inferior to the "world" that is composed of God, others, and self as characterized by the key of the Golden Rule.

How can this be? How can the inclusion of "other" with

self bring greater *Summum Bonum* (greatest good) than "self-only?" How can the going of a "second mile" be advantageous? How can such a rule combine God, others, self, time, eternity, and value in one coherent "world" that solves the problem of evil, happiness, free will, and immortality?

It has been postulated that from a single instance or event a general law cannot be inferred or established (although in one logic system a rule of inference of this nature is allowed). But two points are enough to establish a line, and the self-other pair is enough to establish a veridical relationship. This can be pluralized to a self-others relationship which increases in value, meaning, and satisfaction with multiplication. But how can this be? The loss from pitting self against God and others is greater than any apparent gain in material and power, but the gain from the certainty of a positive relationship with God and others is greater than the apparent loss of going a second mile. A plurality of diverse relations, a heterogeneity of inconsistent, incoherent relationships are handled by one simple rule that exemplifies simple expedience in thinking and economy in net action. What is net action? In a self-only relation, relations with others tends to become circular, redundant, and oscillatory. That is, others have to be subdued time and time again, impositions which have been cast off have to be repeatedly replaced and persuading arguments have to be professed repeatedly, so that the net expenditure for repeated action is greater than the expenditure of going a second mile. Put simply, there is more economy in going two miles by choice and in good will than there is by going many separate, but later, repeated miles by compulsion of necessity (in carrying out an ambition) and in ill will. In other words, if you are dealing with others and are *trying to establish something* you may do so by giving others a double measure of value, service, or satisfaction. If you are dealing with others and are meeting a requirement, you may do so by again giving a double measure. In ancient times a Roman soldier could compel a Jew to carry his pack a mile. If the Jew carried the soldier's pack two miles he might well have made a friend out of an enemy who might never again have asked him to carry his pack.

Objection may be made that this is axiological (concerning values) but not rational. Well then, if the concept of the Golden Rule be abstracted to a systematic rule to qualify it as rational, although axiology is admittedly a branch of philosophy, it may be stated as "Take Half and Give Double." The atomic theory holds that the universe contains atoms which are in constant interaction with each other, one psychological theory holds that an ego is in interaction with an environment, while one social theory holds that people are in constant interaction with one another. The point is interaction. We live in a "give and take" world so to speak. Thus a "Take half and give double" rule would say: "When someone offers you a quantity X, take X/2; if some one requires X of you, give 2X." Since life partly consists in receiving judgment-perverting gifts (although I do not say all gifts are given in that spirit and for that purpose) and partly meeting stipulated impositions and requirements, the former can be handled by taking half while the latter may be handled by giving double.

In practice the results often appear to reduce one to complete poverty, but the moral gain sustains one until matters improve while hope is never extinguished. Viewed in an abstracted form the rule is open to basic questions: Why is it better to take half rather than the whole, and why is it better to give double rather than the required one? With respect to the former, some answers are: Since a gift "perverteth the wise" a half measure retains sociability and some measure of self-control. Also the predetermined rule facilitates decision-making and minimizes loss from quandary and inner debate. With respect to the latter, some answers are: Giving double changes a requirement into a philanthropic action, changes ill will into good will, and facilitates expedient and economical handling of wealth. Thus the positive unity that results from handling problems successfully is applied to other areas with gain in administrative effectiveness and increase in appreciation of possessions and values. As an imaginative case, one might consider a Mr. X who is offered a million dollars as a gift. (Numerous cases like this, but without the use of the proposed rule, have resulted in meaningless marriages, principleless living, and even in suicide, as was the case of a Nobel Prize winner who walked out into the ocean.) If Mr. X takes only $500,000, he refuses $500,000 with the result that he demonstrates an element of self-control, which element can then be used in a judicious disposition of the remaining $500,000. If Mr. X takes the whole $1,000,000 he exercises no self-control and could well squander it in debauchery.

Again, let us consider Mr. X as he applies the "give double" part of the rule to his life. A friend, hearing that Mr. X has received the $500,000, asks him for $1,000. If Mr. X refuses, he will lose a friend, perhaps be driven to a darkened view of life, considering everyone a threat to his fortune, and perhaps also incur an illness in the stress and attending strain. But if Mr. X gives $2,000, the friend will be retained, satisfied, gratified, and even indebted to Mr. X. And besides this, it is unlikely that he will ask for more money. If Mr. X neither refuses to give any money at all nor gives double but gives the $1,000 asked for, the friend may come back repeatedly, at intervals, for $1,000, thus resulting in negative consequences in case of refusal of additional amounts, or the loss of many thousands of dollars in repeated givings, not to mention the question that will probably be in his mind, "Will he ever stop coming back for more?" Thus we see that the giving of $2,000 by Mr. X avoids the negative consequences of refusing to give; also the loss of many thousands of dollars with no assurance of a limit to the losses.

Thus, starting with perhaps nothing, Mr. X can receive $500,000 (this is a presumption of course) while still retaining self-control, self-respect, and a set of values and while still meeting requirements, retaining friends and doing philanthropic works. These results are obtained by an abstraction of the Golden Rule, which may seem to approach a position which is not of self-only solipsism but nonetheless one of enlightened self-interest. And this may be the case. But the abstraction lends itself to the use by one who has the spirit of the Golden Rule as well as the formula, as well as it lends itself to the one who has enlightened self-interest or one who has the formula and mixed motives.

The formula can be used in difficult situations where it is difficult to apply the Golden Rule in its primary spiritual postulation. But whether in rational, abstract application or in warm-hearted, good-willed application, the Golden Rule bears good fruit while constituting a consistent, coherent "world" that builds for a future existence while securing the present existence.

In presenting a discourse that can be applied to material and also to spiritual things a certain length is needed. Although the quality of a concept, idea, or rule may often be shown in a few words, it should be obvious that the principle of the Golden Rule (and "take half and give double") may be applied over a large range.

In the context of philosophical theology and idealism this rule shows the mind to be a spirit that can consider itself and others, has will, but sees that its greatest gain lies in loving, revering, and obeying God and in satisfying in others the desires it finds in itself. Considering others in sympathy, love and, good will causes one to abide in the Truth (the Lord Jesus Christ) which (who) is the Light of the world.

Ordinary reason (Immanuel Kant differentiated "practical" reason from "pure reason." Here there is a similarity but what is meant is reasoning with two interests in mind "self" and "others.") has a range between zero and one, that is, remains within the range of self-interest (others considered if and only if they are fostering that self-interest). The revelation of the Golden Rule gives a range beyond this extending to infinity. Put in homely terms, the ordinary reasoning would be like a *bank account*. The owner would say, "I have so much, I can do so much, buy so much, indulge so much." Whereas reasoning according to the revealed Golden Rule is like an adoption into a great family wherein a man finds a brother in every man, a kinswoman in every girl and woman, heaven as a home and all the earth as a possession, possessed in the sense in which appreciation possesses a thing of beauty or value.

Such a rule allows freedom—freedom to do good, help others, and prevent evil. Such a freedom is restricted to God's will and glory and to man's good, not allowing, however, the practice of evil. Not to be forgotten is the freedom it gives from the consequences of malice, ill will, and the practice of evil if one has and practices these.

Metaphysically and epistemologically this is knowing in a positive sense. One may forget something he did for himself, but not be uncertain nor forget easily something good he did for someone else (for he has no need to repress the memory, nor to be ashamed of it). The Golden Rule is really logical in that a certainty is established and positive inference can be made. Not only this, but absolute predictions (prediction being the desired factor in any system or science) can be made. "Give and it shall be given unto you," "And ye shall have treasure in heaven." "You shall never regret this" are a few. "This act solves a particular problem and makes the world a better place to live in" is another.

This rule opens the eyes to the needs of others. Problems are seen clearly and solutions are obvious. One practicing this rule can turn, wherever he is, to worship God in spirit and in truth. This rule gives harmony to mankind, for a consideration of the plight of others stirs up sympathy for them. The sympathy involved in giving and the appreciation involved in receiving together result in harmony. This of course is increased as more than one, even many, practice the rule.

In the context of the Enlightenment, this rule is the essence of a belief that God may be worshiped by a person's helping his fellowman. Even in a business the rule impels one to sell good merchandise at a just price for the true welfare and satisfaction of the customer and hold him in a bond of good will and friendship. A businessman, following this rule will have very good credit and true success (if success means satisfaction as well as financial profit).

In the face of the criticism of religion, this rule, when practiced properly, offers an irrefutable argument. Such a rule must have a divine origin, and its true practice melts criticism. The rule holds well in affairs of state, as is witnessed by the part of the Declaration of Independence which says: "A decent respect for the opinions of mankind requires that they should declare the causes which impel them to the separation." Such a statement is just and gains a ready audience and a profound consideration.

This rule obtains a respect from rulers and is itself the start of self-government. This rule results in a true nobleness, the nobleness of the children of God. In the light of this rule knowledge and wisdom easily follow. Truly this rule is the essence of what is commonly called the moral sense. One practicing this rule attains unto true virtue. If the rule were diligently followed, Christianity would convert the entire world, for the occasions that have caused divisions within the Church and offenses to those outside the Church would be eliminated. This is offered in reply to those who might doubt the existence of God because Christianity is not universal. However, that very fact bears witness to a characteristic of the rule—its freedom allows for refusal and rejection.

Many aspects of deism seem to have been founded upon this rule. The rule must have a divine origin. Even the giving of the rule to mankind is evidence of God's Providence. Certainly the rule incites man to reason, for a person must consider his own desires, the needs and desires of others, and often how ways and means may be devised to effect the beneficence. Who will deny that the miraculous is seen in practical form in the Golden Rule? One may pray for bread from heaven, but the need is already seen by another who lives by the rule. And is not a needy one, receiving help, inclined to belief in God? Who will deny personality to the One who gave the Golden Rule? Desire, sympathy, consideration, thought, goodness, and compassion, all marks of personality, are required to practice this rule. Would not the Giver of the rule Himself first have these? If the rule is not restricted in application to one man or a few men but is to be applied to all mankind, it thus considers general as well as particular needs and conditions. One critic of religion professed faith in one God, the equality of man, the doing of justice, mercy, and benevolence. He denied the creeds of churches and said his own mind was his church. A genuine practice of the Golden Rule would not be regretted by such a man, nor result in offense at the Redeemer who gave it.

And so for the application of the rule in the context of transcendentalism, evolution (Here a light is shown. Evolution proceeds by progeny. The Golden Rule jumps the gap from self to alien. It is quite unnatural; in fact, it is supernatural, not being practiced naturally by men, not even to mention the animals.), idealism, pragmatism, naturalism, realism, and even in the philosophy of science. The Golden Rule stimulates production of good consequences and the means whereby they may be carried out.

But those in science not living by this rule, but nonetheless seeking fruitfulness and the benefit of mankind under the banner of "progress," lest us say, are faced with the problems that attend any view or way of life that is indifferent to the Creator of man and Nature. Max Weber, in an article called "Science as a Vocation," says: "Every scientific fulfillment raises new questions; it asks to be surpassed and outdated." Also: "In principle, this progress goes on *ad infinitum*." Then again: "Under these internal presuppositions, what is the meaning of science as a vocation, now after all these former illusions, the way to true being, the way to true art; the way to true nature, the way to true God, the way to true happiness, have been dispelled? Tolstoi has given the simplest answer with the words: 'Science is meaningless because it gives no answer to our question, the only question important for us: "What shall we do and how shall we live?"'" Max Weber goes on to mention the contributions that science makes but notes that the world needs a Savior and is troubled by the fact that "today only within the smallest and intimate circles, in personal human situations, in *pianissimo*, that something is pulsating that corresponds to the prophetic *pneuma*, which in former times swept through the great communities like a firebrand, welding them together" (38, pp. 7, 9 in Bibliography). He says further that one can return (to God): "The arms of the old churches are opened widely and compassionately for him," but that: "One way or another he has to bring his intellectual sacrifice—that is inevitable. If he can really do it, we shall not rebuke him. For such an intellectual sacrifice in favor of an unconditional religious devotion is quite a different matter than the evasion of the plain duty of intellectual integrity, which sets in if one lacks the courage to clarify one's own ultimate standpoint and rather facilitates this duty by feeble relative judgments" (38, p. 15 in Bibliography).

This article was written about 1946. Since then great changes have occurred, principally due to changes required in math and science in dealing with nuclear physics. Dr. Vannevar Bush, writing in the May, 1965, issue of *Fortune Magazine*, in the article called "Science Pauses," says: "This is a misconception that scientists can establish a complete set of facts and relations about the universe, all neatly proved, and that on this basis men can securely establish their personal philosophy, their personal religion, free from doubt and error." Also: "On the essential and central core of faith, science will of necessity be silent." Then: "But its silence will be one of humility, not a silence of disdain. A belief may be larger than a fact." Again: "And he can then step beyond to lead men in paths of righteousness and in paths of peace." Finally: "And, with a pause, he will admit a faith" (6, pp. 116, 174 in Bibliography).

Although the view presented here concerning the Golden Rule is a version, the full and exact particulars are found in the New Testament. The presentation there is authoritative. He who truly follows the Scriptures builds upon the Rock of Ages, the Lord Jesus Christ. The desires of science as admitted by Dr. Bush and the Scriptures are one in this: "Righteousness and peace."

Chapter Seven

Biblical Criticism

I. The Defense of the Bible as the Word of the Living God

The Bible speaks of Divine Wisdom (Christ the Wisdom of God) that is from above, men's wisdom, and devilish wisdom ("earthly, sensual, devilish"). These three types of wisdom, from God, of men, and of devils enter into the defense of the Bible as the Word of the Living God; the wisdom from God presenting the truth, men's wisdom presenting half the truth and the devilish wisdom contradicting the truth.

The first instance of the antithesis between God's word and the Devil's word is given in Genesis 2:16, 17; "And the Lord God commanded the man, saying, of every tree of the garden thou mayest freely eat: but of the tree of the knowledge of good and evil, thou shalt not eat of it: for in the day that thou eatest thereof thou shalt surely die," and Genesis 3:1, 4, 5: "Now the serpent was more subtle than any beast of the field which the Lord God had made. And he said unto the woman, Yea, hath God said, Ye shall not eat of every tree of the garden? . . . And the serpent said unto the woman, Ye shall not surely die: for God doth know that in the day ye eat thereof, then your eyes shall be opened, and ye shall be as gods, knowing good and evil." The Devil first questions what God said and then he contradicts it.

Thus in the criticism of the Bible the first line of attack is contradiction and the method of contrary position. The Bible says that man fell from a high state to a lower state. Those proposing the theory of evolution try to show that man went from a low state to a higher state. Thus you have the antithesis "down-up." The Bible shows that man apart from God got and gets worse morally. One near-modern assertion is that man by himself can get morally better. Thus you have another antithesis, "worse-better." God's Word has been confirmed because of the many prophecies it made *before* the events that were fulfilled. Some criticizing the Bible try to shift dates of authorship to a time later than the actual time. Thus you have another antithesis, "before-after." In the writing of the inspired Bible you have man depending upon God. Some criticizing the Bible try to show that one book of the Bible depended upon another book of the Bible and, having already postulated the Bible as being of human origin, to show that man depended upon man. Thus you have the antithesis, "God-dependent and Man-Dependent."

You have some of the devilish wisdom mixed into the wisdom of man but in general man's wisdom presents half of the truth. (You have more antitheses like "miracles are possible—miracles are impossible," "The Bible is the Holy Book—The Bible is the dirtiest book there is," "The Bible is the Word of Truth—It's all a pack of lies," "I believe—I doubt" and others). In this area man seeks to discredit the Bible with respect to historical and textual evidences. One rule is to "divide and conquer." Thus two authors are postulated for Isaiah, two Johns for the Book of Revelation, one John for the Fourth Gospel and another John for the Epistle of John. Epistles are cut into pieces as prologues or endings (or even middle parts) as having been added later, differences are noted but agreements ignored, Peter set against Paul, the Book of Acts set against the Epistles of Paul, Pauline style set against un-Pauline style, and motive set apart from consequences.

When doctrines are attacked divisions are attempted, like

denying the inspiration of the Holy Spirit and the divinity of Jesus to produce a division in the Trinity. When facts are attacked part of the evidence is often omitted to make them "contingent," or to "neutralize" them ("not necessarily so" or "maybe yes, maybe no.")

More subtle techniques include allegorizing (where the fallacy "each to all"—"one part is allegory, therefore all parts are allegories," is committed) and sophistry (where equivocation is used, the using of a term in two senses and terms or premises are turned against each other producing a contradiction because one term or premise is used in the sense of identity and the other is used in the sense of *existential import*, that is, of existence). Other techniques include the indirect "refutation" (The Bible is not true but its nice to pretend and act "as if" it were true) and the "oblique" attack (Paul, the Jew, had a different kind of Christianity and his teaching could not be practiced. For instance, his prohibition against marriage . . . if that were followed the whole church would die out in one generation. And emphasis [in effect] on grace and spirituality did not contribute to the survival of the Church; it needed [in effect] law for government and survival).

Before modern archeology many facts were denied as being true as recorded in the Bible: It was asserted that there was no writing in the time of Moses; the Jews never were in captivity in Egypt and many cities listed in the Bible never existed; many similar things were asserted concerning the New Testament. Now, however, after much archeological work, many of the denied facts have been proved true. New papyri and the Dead Sea Scrolls have confirmed these things.

II. *Personal Factors Affecting the Receipt of the Truth*

A. *Apathy*

Jesus said: "For this people's heart is waxed gross, and their ears are dull of hearing, and their eyes they have closed;

lest at any time they should see with their eyes, and hear with their ears, and should understand with their heart, and should be converted, and I should heal them" (20, Matt. 13: 15).

B. *Inherent Nature*

All unborn-again men partake of the fallen nature of Adam. Some, however, partake to a greater extent of some of the more negative aspects of that nature. Again, Jesus said: "Give not that which is holy unto the dogs, neither cast ye your pearls before swine, lest they trample them under their feet, and turn again and rend you" (20, Matt. 7:6). Thus a person's inner nature will affect his reaction to truth.

C. *Will*

Jesus said again: "O Jerusalem, Jerusalem, thou that killest the prophets, and stonest them which are sent unto thee, how often would I have gathered thy children together, even as a hen gathereth her chickens under her wings, and ye would not" (20, Matt. 23:37). The will affects our selection of things we consider important and our "reasons" for doing so. Unfortunately, people inside the church are also affected. Illingworth gave a very good statement concerning this:

> Whoever indeed will consider the nature of man, or will consult obvious experience, shall find that in all practical matters our will or appetite hath a mighty influence on our judgment of things; causing men with great attention to regard that which they affect, and carefully to mark all reasons making for it; but averting from that which they dislike, and making them to overlook the arguments which persuade it; whence men generally do suit their opinions to their inclinations; warping to that side where their interest doth lie, or to which their complexion, their humor, their passions, their pleasure, their ease doth

sway them; so that almost any notion will seem true, which is profitable, which is safe, which is pleasant, or anywise grateful to them; that notion false, which in any respect doth cross them; very few can abstract their minds from such considerations, or embrace pure truth, divested of them; and those few who do so, must therein most employ their will, by strong efforts of voluntary resolution and patience disengaging their minds from those clogs and biasses. This is particularly notorious in men's adherence to parties, divided in opinion, which is so regulated by that sort of causes, that if you do mark what any man's temper is, and where his interest doth lie, you may easily prognosticate on what side he will be, and with what degree of seriousness of vigor, of zeal he will cleave thereto; a timorous man you may be almost sure will be on the safer side; a covetous man will bend to that party where gain is to be had; an ambitious man will close with the opinion passing in court; a careless man will comply with the fashion; affection arising from education or prejudice will hold others stiff; few do follow the results of impartial contemplation. All faith, therefore, even in common things, may be deemed voluntary, no less than intellectual; and Christian faith is especially such, as requiring thereto more application of soul, managed by choice, than any other; whence the ancients, in their description of it, do usually include this condition, supposing it not to be a bare assent of the understanding but a free consent of the will: Faith, saith Clemens Alexandrinus, is a spontaneous acceptance, and compliance with divine religion. (Barrow, Serm. on Apost. Creed, ii. p. 58, 24 in Bibliography)

This is something all men are subject to. Notwithstanding, men outside the church have Christ as an example of one referring to principle rather than arbitrariness, to the will of God rather than to His own will. (Even people in the church often fall short in this, praying for what they want and doing what they want to do instead of praying "Father, help us do Thy will")

D. Qualification of Apologists

While a person may have a desire to strike out blindly at all that opposes the will of God and that criticizes the Bible, Christians are admonished to take heed. Then Jesus said unto them, "Yet a little while is the light with you. Walk while ye have the light, lest darkness come upon you; for he that walketh in darkness knoweth not whither he goeth. While ye have the Light, believe in the Light, that ye may be children of Light" (John 12:35, 36a).

Also, because the Christian is of the truth he can and is admonished to give a "reason" for his hope. "But sanctify the Lord God in your hearts, and be ready to give an answer to every man that asketh you a reason of the hope that is in you with meekness and fear" (I Pet. 3:15). God is no respecter of persons (Acts 10:34). He is the Saviour of all men (I Tim. 4:10), and Christians are admonished to refer to a universal standard "every man's conscience." "But have renounced the hidden things of dishonesty, not walking in craftiness, nor handling the Word of God deceitfully; but by manifestation of the Truth commending ourselves to every man's conscience in the sight of God" (II Cor. 4:2). Therefore in a situation where critical views are opposed some universal standard must be agreed upon. Men from two different colleges intended to have a debate. They could not agree on the "ground rules," on the "generic" statement, so they could not hold the debate. Proof, or argumentative conviction or persuasion, requires an initial standard in terms of which all other statements are judged. In criticism, arguments are judged as valid or invalid. The word comes from the Latin word *valere*, which means "to be strong." Thus arguments can be judged as strong, but also as of correct form. Thus a logical consideration of the issues brought up by Biblical criticism involves reference to validity and fallaciousness.

III. The Rules of Logic

Francis Bacon wrote the *Novum Organum*. One of the things he was trying to do was to correct what he believed to be errors in scholastic science. He noted things that affect the mind itself which "plunge us into hasty generalizations and prevent our seeing the exceptions to them" (25, p. 601 in Bibliography). He made four classifications of things of this nature and called them "idols."

> *The Idols of the Tribe;* The human understanding is of its own nature prone to suppose the existence of more order in the world than it finds; *The Idols of the Cave* take their rise in the peculiar constitution, mental or bodily, of each individual; also in education, habit, and accident. But the *Idols of the Market Place* are most troublesome of all, idols which have crept into the understanding through the alliance of words and names. But the *Idols of the Theatre* are not innate, nor do they steal into the understanding secretly, but are plainly impressed and received into the mind from the play-books of philosophical systems and the perverted rules demonstration. (25, pp. 601-603 in Bibliography)

But while these things may be true to a greater or lesser degree, since the will is most basic and will guides the interpretation of these things, recourse must be had to impartial logical rules. Herbert L. Searles notes that the primary possible logical relations between any two propositions (contradiction, contrariety, subcontratiety, superimplication, subimplication, equivalence, and independence) are based upon the three laws (or principles) of thought, the Law of Identify (Every entity is what it is,) the Law of Noncontradiction (an entity cannot both be and not be at the same time and place), and the Law of Excluded Middle. (An entity either is or is not at the same time and place, 33, pp. 89, 90 in Bibliography. He also gives a good classification of fallacies.

If *great care* is taken to analyze *each* issue and criticism made against the Bible many will be shown to be fallacious. It is admitted that the textual evidence is not such as it would be if the very original documents were extant. Many of the original letters probably suffered greatly from use, but some may be buried with some early Christian in a catacomb. However, when the evidence allows of a plausible deduction based on secondary sources, logical rules can be used. If a person revolts against such a consideration, the situation can revert to predictions upon will and "I like it," or "I don't like it." (One fact remains. If a person looks into the existing evidence there is enough to convict him of being a sinner. If he rejects Jesus' words he will be judged by them nonetheless on the last day.)

IV. Basic Issues and Criticisms of the Old Testament

The first point of attack is against the Five Books of Moses. Mention is made of statements in the last part concerning Moses' burial and the charge that Moses did not write that part and that hence he did not write any of it. This is the "each to all" fallacy (hasty generalization and the confusion of collectives).

It is alleged that Moses got the material for the "Five Books" from Egypt, Babylonia, and other countries around him in his time. In order to prove such a statement the person making it must examine all the evidence, most of which is gone, talk with the people who lived in all those countries at that time, and explore the realm of the invisible. If he cannot do this he must take a step backward and say: "It is *possible* that Moses got the material for the Five Books from the surrounding countries in his time." The "gods" of the surrounding countries were to be feared, but the First Commandment commands love for God. God was not presented to Moses as a material idol. He is Spirit. He is the Living God. If someone points to the Code of Hammurabi as the source of the Mosaic Law, one cannot deny that the Creator of all men allowed men to have a code less in perfection than the Mosaic Law and this agrees with the Genesis assertion that Adam fell. Imperfect legends of the Flood do not detract from the Genesis flood account but support it, showing that men had the idea of the true account in their legends.

The account of the serpent changing (or being given a changed form) is nothing to disparage, seeing that many parasites now alive change their form many times, like the liver fluke (11, p. 71 in Bibliography). It is not necessary to go through all the "Mistakes of Moses" seeing that archeology has found the ruins of Sodom, as well as many other cities, confirmed the date of the captivity as 597 B.C. (21, p. 9 in Bibliography), and confirmed the Old Testament in many points. But seeing that the text of the Old Testament has been carefully preserved and handed down and the Jews as a race have been historically in existence since the time of Moses, never having renounced the Old Testament, *the text is as valid now* as it was when it was first written. This being the case and both the captivity of the Jews in Egypt and their stay in Canaan having been confirmed by historical evidence, no one can logically deny that the Jews were released contrary to nature and hence supernaturally, that they were taken across the Red Sea contrary to nature, and hence supernaturally, and that they were sustained contrary to nature (little food and water for three and a half million people), and hence supernaturally. And not only this but the prophecies which were made and fulfilled in Old Testament times are evidence.

V. *Basic Issues in the New Testament*

Before going into these issues it should be noted that the fact that Jesus Christ fulfilled the Old Testament prophecies about Himself qualified Him to speak as a historical witness concerning all the rest of the Old Testament. He said Adam existed, and there is not one living man on earth who has the context-corroborated, time-honored character that Jesus has and who can contradict Him. The logical possibilities concerning Him are: (1) He was myth and never existed; (2) He was the greatest deceiver who ever lived; (3) He was mentally ill and deluded; or (4) He was what He claimed to be. The evidence overwhelmingly falls into the last category.

But with respect to the basic issues in the New Testament it may be said that they fall into two categories at least: external-evidence-related issues or internal-evidence-related issues. There exists at this present time the Codex Vaticanus and the Codex Sinaiticus both from the mid-fourth century. There exists many earlier copies of New Testament books and fragments of the New Testament books. Also there now exists many early documents written by the early Church Fathers which quote passages from the New Testament books. Bruce Metzger notes a laborious work that shows the great quantity of the quotations:

> In addition to the previously mentioned *apparatus critici* that contains evidence from the Fathers, reference may also be made to the indexes of biblical citations in the writings of the Fathers. During the past century Dean J. Burgon, that doughty defender of the Textus Receptus, combed through many Greek and Latin folios of the Fathers, marking New Testament quotations in the margins. Then Burgon's assistants extracted the passages (some 86,439 quotations!), arranged them in scriptural sequence, and placed them in sixteen huge scrap books, which today are in the British Museum. Another index, confined to the writings of St. Augustine was prepared last century by that polymatic scholar Paul de Lagarde, who with the help of his wife assembled nearly 30,000 quotations made by Augustine from the New Testament. This handwritten index is now in the University Library at Gottingen. (29, pp. 382, 383 in Bibliography)

The early church wrestled with the problem of which Scriptures are inspired and which are not. In the fifth century the New Testament canon was established. The people of that day were certainly better qualified than the people of this day to determine which Scriptures were canonical. They were closer to the time origin and were disposed, by suffering and commitment, to serious concern and investigation with respect to the matter.

When, however, modern-day critics attack the New Testament, the "general" issues may be put into three statements, as noted by H. E. Dana:

1. The Historical Reliability of the Literary Sources of Christianity.
2. The Basal Motives Underlying the Literature of Christianity.
3. The Claim of Christianity Upon the best Intelligence. (8, pp. 14ff. in Bibliography.)

Because, as mentioned above, the textual evidences are secondary, they must be approached by rational inquiries and assertions in many respects. Dana again notes some very important distinctions that critics should make:

1. Between Facts and the Interpretations of Facts.
2. Between The Essentially Historical and The Essentially Theological.
3. Between the Essential Content of Thought and the Incidental Form of Thought. (8, pp. 15f. in Bibliography)

When the particular books of the New Testament are examined, they are sometimes treated in groups such as the Synoptic Gospels, the Gospel of John, Luke, Acts, the general epistles, the epistles of Paul, and so on. In considering the Synoptic Gospels the chief problem is stated with respect to the *agreement* and *disagreement* of materials in the three respective Gospels. A suggested solution was proposed by the postulation of a hypothetical 'Q" source.

One problem in Matthew that was criticized was the fact that in Matthew 9:9 and 10:2, 3 he is called Matthew and in Mark 2:14 and Luke 5:27 he is called Levi. This difference is played up but the agreement of contexts is ignored. In all three texts the sequence of events is identical: The account of the healing of a man afflicted with palsy is followed by Matthew's "call," which is immediately followed by the occurrence of a feast given by the publican who was "called." The events in each Gospel equal each other and therefore Matthew equals Levi.

In Mark, a problem was raised with respect to the last verses in chapter sixteen from 9 to 20. Some postulate that they were added by someone other than Mark because of the change in emotional sense ("for they were afraid"—"Now when Jesus was risen early the first day of the week") and, seemingly the two assertions with respect to seeing Jesus ("He goeth before you into Galilee: there shall ye see Him," and "Now when Jesus was risen early the first day of the week, He appeared first to Mary Magdalene"). But it should be noted that verse 8 was and still is a general statement. In verse 9 an appearance is noted; in verse 12 another appearance is noted; in verse 14 another appearance is noted. Finally the ascension of the Lord is noted. If a person notices, he will see that in verses 1 to 8 it is Mary who is addressed. He will also see that in verses 9 to 11 it again is Mary who is addressed. So then the two sections are related. They have that common tie. But with respect to 9-11 and 12-13 it will be noted that they have in common the fact that they are both accounts of Jesus' appearances. But this is true with respect to 9-11 and 14-18 so that there is a common feature there too. Thus while it is possible that Mark waited after writing the first part to add the other parts, it is still in any case logical to assume that it was indeed Mark who made the additions. Otherwise the logical possibility that one person for each section made additions (that is, four persons), is open. But the theme for the whole chapter is the same; "The post-resurrection appearances of Jesus." This is the climax and most important part of the whole Gospel. Why would Mark not be inclined to include it?

Because no name is given in Luke for the authorship, some room is left open for criticism. But when Luke and Acts are compared, a logical analysis reduces the authorship to Luke. Michael Wierman quotes and notes the analysis made by E. F. Harrison in his Introduction to the New Testament:

> Harrison believes that by a process of elimination the author of the "we" sections and hence the book of Acts and Luke can be determined. (4, p. 196 in Bibliography) Because the Prison Epistles were written from Rome by Paul, the author that we are seeking would logically be among his companions mentioned in those books. Harrison lists these names: Epaphras, Epaphroditus, Timothy, Tychicus, Aristarchus, Mark, Jesus called Justus, Demas and Luke. He continues saying, Of these Epaphroditus did not arrive in the company of Paul, hence could not have described the sea voyage. Tychicus, Timothy and Mark are ruled out because they are all mentioned at some point in the Book of Acts in the third person. Demas later deserted the apostle, making the identification dubious. Further, there is no tradition in his favor as author. Two remain—Jesus called Justus and Luke. Since there is no indication that the former was with Paul during the events reported in the 'we' sections, and since patristic testimony to his authorship is lacking Luke only is left. (4, pp. 196, 197 Harrison) ([37, p. 4 in Bibliography])

One of the issues with respect to the Gospel of John is the question of authorship. David Skates notes that Bultmann had denied that John was the author becuase of Mark 10:39: "John the son of Zebedee must have been killed by the Jews very early, as Mark 10:39 shows, and as is indicated by several witnesses of the ancient Church" (3, p. ll; 34, p. 8 in Bibliography). Here is an example of misinterpretation. It is written: " . . . And Jesus said unto them, ye shall indeed drink of the cup that I drink of; and with the baptism that I am baptized withal shall ye be baptized" (Mark 10:39). There is no indication of when the time would be that John would drink of the cup of death. There is a real *non sequitur* fallacy.

Another point of criticism with respect to the authorship of John is the fact that the disciple uses the impersonal form of referring to himself. Actually it is the Holy Spirit that said "This is the disciple which testifieth of these things: and we know that his testimony is true" (John 21:24). This is like lawyers saying: "If it please the court." After the Spirit has testified through the apostle he speaks as a man in the last verse (a born again man of course): "And there are also many other things which Jesus did, the which, if they should be written every one, I suppose that even the world itself could not contain the books that should be written. Amen" (John 21:25). The critic creates a dilemma. If the author names himself, this is grounds for a pseudonymity charge because the false apostle is trying to add authority to the text. The Apostle would not be so self-assertive. If on the other hand the author speaks of himself indirectly, he is not an Apostle because the Apostle would be well known and would not have had to make an allusion in indirect form to himself. If a name is used the writing is nonapostolic, and if a name is not used then the writing is nonapostolic. Of course no one writer-critic will use the two assertions together, but a group of critics can and have used the false dilemma on the New Testament as a whole.

When criticism is leveled at the Book of Romans certain problems are found. Mike Houston presents a good statement of many of the problems:

> Although the authenticity of the Book of Romans cannot be questioned, textual difficulties throw some question on certain sections of the Epistle. The doxology of 16:25-27 is likewise omitted from some texts, found after chapter fourteen in others, and in one manuscript is

placed between chapters 15 and 16. The benediction of 16:24 has poor documentation, and 1:7 and 1:15 are omitted by a few authorities. Form critics have also suggested the possibility that 13:1-7; 3:25-26; and 16:17-20 are later interpolations into the text. These questions must be dealt with in order to establish the original form of the book. These problems will be presented in order and possible solutions will be suggested. (23, p. 11 in Bibliography)

The difference is interpreted to mean that other persons or one other person other than the Apostle Paul (actually the Holy Spirit) handled the text. Mike Houston quoted C. H. Dodd to show the point that the Apostle Paul could have made the changes:

> No one doubts that Paul wrote xv-xvi. The question is whether he wrote the short recension, and expanded it later, or whether he wrote the long recension, which was later cut down. (23, p. 11 in Bibliography)

In the Corinthian correspondence a few problems arise. The biggest of these have to do with the question of whether or not they are complete, unified documents or composites of a number of smaller letters. One letter is lost and some try to find it in Second Corinthians 6:14-7:1, because it deals with a warning against being unequally yoked together with unbelievers, and First Corinthians speaks of a previous (lost) epistle in which Paul says: "I wrote unto you in an epistle not to company with fornicators" (5:9). However, the Apostle's thought runs in this wise: He exhorts them "not to receive the grace of God in vain." He mentions things relating to the receiving of the grace of God, stating that God has heard them, "For He Saith, I have heard thee . . . " (6:1a). and that they are not to give offences. He tells them they are straitened in their own bowels (6:11), and instead of apparently *digressing* in 6:14-7:1, he explains the source of their being "straitened," that is, improper fellowship. He is telling them that if they have fellowship with darkness (evil), that they will be straitened, hamper, hindered, and the like. He admonishes them to avoid this and cleanse themselves in spirit and body (7:1) In the very next verse, 7:2, he continues on the theme of fellowship, (the proper fellowship), and wants them to receive him (and the other workers and Apostles). The point is this: The apparent "digression" can be interpreted as strange, foreign, and discontinuous with the context and hence as an "insertion" by another person other than the author. *Rather*, it is an explanation, a clarification, a note within the text and that by the author and not someone else because it is consonant with the theme in that context, "fellowship."

In the Book of Galatians some take great liberties in interpreting it or rather, in the Book of Galatians we find an "instance" where liberties of interpretation are taken, and that chiefly in "modern" times. Jack Burch notes some of the objections and gives a reply:

II. The Pauline authorship of Galatians has been doubted by only a few critics, primarily Bruno Bauer, A. D. Loman, A. Pierson, R. Steck, and Von Manen.
A. Great difference is found even among those who deny the Pauline authorship.
1. Pierson said the epistle originated with a liberal group of Jews.
2. Steck traced it to a Pauline school.
3. Von Manen said the letter began in the circle of Marcionites.
Each of the above hold to a late (second century) date for the epistle.
4. Bruno Bauer and the radical Dutch critics in 1850 concluded Galatians was a compilation by a Paulinist.

B. Shaw summarizes the views of Von Manen, a strong opponent of the Pauline authorship.

1. There are relations in the Epistle so difficult to understand that we must conclude it is untrustworthy.
2. The religious development described could not have occurred in so short a time. Some of these are:

    a. The doctrine and ethical ideas.
    b. The substratum of Old Paulinism.
    c. The form of Christianity described is older.

III. Some answers to the above objections.

A. This type of criticism is dominated by an overly rigid rationalistic theory of development.

B. This tends to create history rather than study it.

C. By this principle of criticism almost all "history" becomes suspect.

D. It is almost impossible to conceive of a forger creating the Acts-Galatians problem relative to the visits to Jerusalem. (5, pp. 1, 2 in Bibliography)

Notice that in II, A, 3, all hold for late dates; here is the trick of manipulating time to move the document away from the time the real author wrote it in order to leave room to postulate another author. This is an effort to eliminate Apostolic authorship. Notice also in II, B, 1, that the fallacy of Argumentum ad Ignorantiam, appeal to ignorance, is used. The invalid assertion is made that: "I don't understand it, therefore it is untrustworthy." Notice also in II, B, 2, a, that "doctrinal and ethical ideas" are said to have "developed" over a period of time, not having been the same from the beginning. This stratagem aims at contradicting the assertion in Galatians 1:8: "But though we, or an angel from heaven, preach any other gospel unto you than that which we have preached unto you, let him be accursed." This is doubly asserted in the next verse where the Apostle uses the word "received." In all three objections (II, B, 2, a.b.c) the idea is the same: Divide and contradict; "old-new, therefore untrustworthy." Whereas the Apostle clearly asserts: The same and keep it the same.

And so it is on throughout the whole New Testament. Some critics examine the evidence, then use fallacious arguments to interpret the evidence. It is true that one Gospel mentions Jesus' having been taken to the Temple when He was eight days old and another Gospel does not; that one Gospel says He was taken to Nazareth (Matt. 2:13-15 and Luke 2:21, 22, 39). Omission in one is not contradiction of the other. The two Gospels complement, not contradict, each other. It is true that the timing may have been close, but only if the critics could show contradicting timing (such as the trip into Egypt and then the visit to the Temple) could it be said that the Gospels contradict each other.

Thus as a whole it may be seen that there are some difficulties but that these may be explained as complementary rather than contradictory. No doctrine is contradicted by one part of the New Testament, in fact, none are; that is, none of the original documents. But the copies corroborate each other in small details such as the kind of fish that the boy brought to Jesus when the multitude was fed, the medical language used by Luke, the pool of Bethesda, customs, and many other things that give more confirmation than any document can have that is over two hundred years old. John says that there were many other things that Jesus did that were not recorded, which if they were recorded would make a great library "not even the world itself could contain the books that should be written" (21:25). So when all the evidence is considered it may be clearly stated that the Christ event could not have been inserted into the historical setting of the time of Caesar Augustus, Cyrenius, and Pontius Pilate with all the people and places involved so as to account for all the corroborating details that mathematically would be astronomical. Considering the time span of the Biblical record, the prophecies foretold and fulfilled, the character of Jesus, the martyrs, the church, changed lives, archeology, early Christian writings that contain over 86,000 quotations from the New Testament, and all the other evidence, the fallacious arguments of the sophists are shown to be invalid and the Bible is shown to be coherent, consistent, and enduring. It is shown to be what it claims to be, the Word of the Living God. (A computer programmed with data like this computed that the Bible has one author.)

Chapter Eight

The Inspiration of the Scriptures

I. The Meaning of the Statement That the Scriptures Are Inspired of God

Genesis 1:2, a, says: "And the spirit of God moved upon the face of the waters." Jesus said to Nicodemus: "The wind bloweth where it listeth, and thou hearest the sound thereof, but canst not tell whence it cometh and whither it goeth: so is every one that is born of the Spirit" (John 3:8). Matthew: 3 16, 17 says: "And Jesus, when He was baptized, went up straightway out of the water: and lo, the heavens were opened unto Him, and He saw the Spirit of God descending like a dove, and lighting upon Him: and lo a voice from heaven, saying, This is My beloved Son, in whom I am well pleased."

Now one definition of the word "meaning" predicates upon the "fixedness" of the "intention" of the statement. The above Scriptures intend to show that the Spirit can "move," appear like a "dove," and "speak." The Spirit "searches" the deep things of God (I Cor. 2:10, 11). "Thy Word is Truth" (John 17:17). The Spirit of Truth guides: "Howbeit when he, the Spirit of Truth, is come, he will guide you into all Truth; for he shall not speak of himself; but whatsoever he shall hear, that will he speak: and he will show you things to come. He shall glorify Me: for he shall receive of mine and shall show it unto you" (John 16:13, 14).

When Jesus was before Pilate, He said: "To this end was I born, and for this cause came I into the world, that I should bear witness unto the Truth. Every one that is of the Truth heareth my voice" (John 18:37). "Pilate therefore said unto Him, What is Truth?" (John 18:38a). On the Day of Pentecost the Spirit came. There was a sound as of a mighty rushing wind, "and there appeared unto them cloven tongues like as of fire, and it sat upon each of them. And they were all filled with the Holy Ghost, and began to speak with other tongues, as the Spirit gave them utterance" (Acts 2:3,4). Not only did the Apostles speak with other tongues, but the people to whom they later spoke heard the message in their own languages: "And how hear we every man in our own tongues, wherein we were born?" (Acts 2:8) Now the truth is not limited to language but many gifts are given by the Spirit:

> Now there are diversities of gifts, but the same Spirit. And there are differences of administration but the same Lord. And there are diversities of operations, but it is the same God which worketh all in all. But the manifestation of the Spirit is given to every man to profit withal. For to one is given by the Spirit the word of wisdom; to another the word of knowledge by the same Spirit; to another faith by the same spirit; to another the gifts of healing by the same Spirit; to another the working of miracles; to another prophecy; to another discerning of spirits; to another divers kinds of tongues; to another the interpretation of tongues, But all these worketh that one and the selfsame Spirit, dividing to every man severally as he will. (I Cor. 12:4-11)

Now when God spoke to Moses and the Prophets He spoke directly to them. He wrote words with His own fingers (Ex. 31:18) and fingers (or fingers that He caused) (Dan. 5:5), but He also spoke the words to His messengers and let them write them. The Biblical record contains God's propositional prescriptions but also true witness of events, places and the words and deeds of men and women. Note that the messengers were "holy" men: "For the prophecy came not in old time by the will of man: but holy men of God spoke as they were moved by the Holy Ghost" (I Pet. 1:20). Now the manner and the degree of this "moving" of the Holy Ghost has been questioned. Also the manner and degree of the preserving of the physically written text, the proclamation of that word to men, their reception and response to that proclamation, their understanding of the proclamation, and the carrying out of that proclamation in their lives by the Holy Ghost has been questioned. How much and to what degree did the will and personality of the messenger express itself in the text? The text shows personal "style" involved in the different books yet the Truth was given; given as ten witnesses to an action can bear witness and tell the truth, the whole truth, and nothing but the truth speaking in different tones of voice at different rates of speeds, with different degrees of emotion. This would also happen when the truth is written instead of being spoken.

Some view the writings as of a mechanical inspiration wherein the Spirit moved the messengers hand for them just as if the Spirit used a pen without a human hand. Some see the inspiration varying as the degree to which the messenger was holily descended.

When we come to the New Testament, we see the perfection of all such considerations in Jesus, the Word made flesh, so that there was no hindrances and He could say: "Ye have heard it hath been said by them of old time . . . but I say unto you . . . " (Matt. 5:33, 34). However, since it was the Apostles who wrote down what Jesus said, and wrote the Epistles, the same old considerations of personality and style were raised by critics. Yet the same reasoning applies to them. They were witnesses speaking the Truth and writing the Truth. Yet they had personalities; but the important point is that they were "born again." They put on Christ, were baptized "into

Christ" and had "the mind of Christ." The Holy Spirit brought the remembrance of details to them just as Jesus said he would. Jesus also said: "For the Holy Ghost shall teach you in the same hour what ye ought to say" (Luke 12:12) and also: "For it is not ye that speak, but the Spirit of your Father which speaketh in you" (Matt. 10:20). The Spirit can speak directly through a person or teach a person what to say.

Some try to avoid problems related to a "mechanical" inspiration by posing a "dynamic" theory: "The so-called dynamic theory brings us somewhat nearer the Truth, though it too falls short. This theory is a reaction against the mechanical, and affirms that the human qualities of the writers are not superseded, but are cleansed, strengthened, and employed by the Divine Author" (19, p. 834 in Bibliography). The same article gives a summary view thus:

a. It is men, not directly the writings, that were inspired.

b. When we say that a writer is Divinely inspired, we mean that as he writes he is under the influence of the Holy Spirit.

c. Inspiration is primarily a spiritual gift, and only secondarily a mental one. (19, p. 835 in Bibliography)

This accommodates the feelings of some critics thinking as scholars, mindful of some difficulties and not as inspired as were the original Apostles. The chief difference lies in a completely committed life that has the love of God and wishes to do the will of God, in spite of any selfish interest and so used by the Person of the Holy Spirit. The Holy Spirit is a Person. He can be resisted, grieved, and quenched. When this is done his work can be interpreted as "influence." People are urged to "stir up" the gift that is within them (2 Tim. 1:6), to walk "in the Truth," "walk in the Spirit," to "sow to the Spirit" and "perfect holiness in the fear of God" but the Apostles were doing all these fully when they spoke and wrote for God.

Various interests among other things influence the interpretation of the degree to which the Scriptures are inspired by the Holy Spirit. E. H. Browne and C. J. Ellicott ask the pertinent question: "All spiritual enlightenment is derived from (or by) the Divine Spirit: but is all derived in the same way?" (4, p. 5 in Bibliography). L. Gausen writes:

> It is human and fallible, say you, only in a certain measure; but who shall define this measure? If it be true that man, in putting his baneful impress upon it, have left the stains of humanity there, who shall determine the depth of that impression, and the number of those stains? (13, p. 7 in Bibliography)

Thus questions are raised to match the difficulties attending the present state of the text of the Bible. The New Testament itself speaks of "seed" falling into four different types of soil and also of men who refused to come to a marriage feast because of occupation with various interests. John M. Gibson sees faith as a factor in the determination:

> The outward authority may bring within sight of the Truth, but it is the inner vision which sees it. That inner vision is faith. And the essence of faith is not a blind easy-going assent to the statement of some person or persons regarded as an authority external to our own minds and hearts; it is an energy of mind, and heart, and soul going out to the Truth, especially to Him who is the Truth, and accepting it as bringing its own credentials direct from the Father of lights. (14 in Bibliography)

Now the New Testament says that faith comes by hearing and hearing by the Word (Rom. 10:17). But other things enter into the picture. Drawing by the Father is mentioned (John 6:44). Also repentance in order that one might believe is mentioned (Matt. 21:30). The word is Spirit and Life ("The words that I speak unto you, they are spirit and they are life" (John 6:63).

There is no doubt in the mind of a Christian that the words of the Bible are inspired until a critic points out difficulties. There are a few, but Harry Rimmer says that some are fancies:

> Higher criticism however, is the attempt to repudiate the text upon the basis of fancied errors in its structure.
>
> The higher critical method is to presume that the Bible contains error and fallacy and then seek to establish that premise. (32, pp. 26, 27 in Bibliography)

Some, it appears, deliberately seek to discredit the Scriptures. One trick is to charge the Bible with fallacy and then use fallacy in an effort to prove it. One fallacy (not a serious one) is seen in the charge: "The Bible takes all of the fun out of life." Not only is this an instance of the fallacy of "each to all" (some fun out of life, therefore all fun out of life) but also it contradicts the Scripture: "For the kingdom of heaven is not meat and drink, but righteousness and peace and joy in the Holy Ghost" (Rom. 14:17).

René Pache holds that inspiration was given in a compulsive way:

> Inspiration was given at times in a wholly compulsive way.
> At times the author did not even suspect the divine action brought to bear upon him.
> In essence, divine inspiration knows no degrees. (31, pp. 54, 55 in Bibliography)

The original texts were inspired, no doubt, and critics should allow for this and for inspired manuscripts that were entirely lost (some by deliberate burning). Sometimes a statement is made, "Paul had no knowledge of this." That cannot be proved. The apparent difficulties related to copies of originals cannot disprove inspiration. Instances not requiring the effect of the whole, yet having force, are seen in prophecies. John Davidson points out the admitted requirements for valid prophecy:

> First, the human promulgation of the prophecy prior to the event. Secondly, the clear and palpable fulfillment of it. Lastly, the nature of the event itself, if, when the prediction of it was given, it lay remote from human view, and was such as could not be foreseen by any supposable effort of reason, or be deducted upon principles of calculation derived from probability or experience. (9 in Bibliography)

The mathematical probability of Jesus being the Messiah by virtue of having fulfilled thirty-three major prophecies and many minor allusions in the Old Testament is 10^{180} or 10^{181} to one (ten to the 180th power). The chances that fulfillment of prophecies are accidental are about one to 10^{180} or 10^{181} (the inverse of the other figure). The total product is composed of factors each of which are products of such things as the number of years elapsed until the prophecy was fulfilled times the possible instances at the time of the fulfillment.

The various views of the degrees and kinds of inspiration have been summarized fairly well by Basil Manly, listing "mechanical inspiration" (no room for human activity); "partial inspiration" (emotion and narrative excluded, some things left to the individual, ideas given but not specific language or illustrations); "different degrees of inspiration" (some parts more than others, some less completely than others related to "the amount and nature of the divine control supposed to be exercised"); "natural inspiration" (like unto the inspiration of geniuses and poets); and "Universal inspiration" (the "personal influence of the Holy Spirit"), and "plenary inspiration." ("It is that the Bible as a whole is the Word of God, so that in every part of Scripture there is both infallible Truth and divine authority.") (28 in Bibliography)

With respect to the difficulties again Torrey says:

> The fact that you cannot solve a difficulty does not prove that it cannot be solved, and the fact that you cannot answer an objection does not prove at all that it cannot be answered. (2)
>
> The seeming defects of the Book are exceedingly insignificant when put in comparison with its many and marvelous excellencies. (3)
>
> The sixth thing that may be said about the difficulties in the Bible is, they have far more weight with the superficial readers of the Bible than with profound students of the Bible. (36, in Bibliography)

Ferguson in an article which was first a lecture for the Abilene Christian College Lectures says: "God who once spoke still speaks through His written word. That word must ever remain for us a living voice. (12, in Bibliography)

III. Conclusion

The Scriptures bear witness to the problem of sin and God's pronouncement against it, first to the Jews and then to those who have become the sons of God by the new birth in the Lord Jesus Christ. When all the problems have been considered with respect to the question of the meaning of the "inspiration" of the Scriptures, one last consideration should be made. The Scriptures should be examined for propositional statements that are made with respect to condemning sin and dealing with it, with respect to instructions of how to attain immortality and eternal life, and lastly with respect to what the Scriptures say with respect to the Holy Spirit himself.

The Scriptures reveal the nature and characteristics of the Spirit (I Cor. 12 et. at.), the work and operation of the Spirit and even a test for the Holy Spirit: "Hereby know ye the Spirit of God: Every spirit that confesseth Jesus Christ is come in the flesh is of God" (I John 4:2), and "Wherefore I give you to understand, that no man speaking by the Spirit of God calleth Jesus accursed: and that no man can say that Jesus is the Lord, but by the Holy Ghost."

Anyone studying the Scriptures with respect to the meaning of the "inspiration" of the Scriptures should consider how the Spirit worked in the lives of the Messengers of God as well as what was written. It should be remembered that the Word of God is not bound (2 Tim. 2:9), but Living and active (Heb. 4:12). Omission of complete continuous details is no reason to conclude contradiction, but if one resists the Holy Spirit he will not have the Truth in him and cannot make true analyses and true deductions. If one seeks God's will he will know that the Apostles were speaking from God: "We are of God: he that knoweth God heareth us; he that is not of God heareth not us. Hereby know we the Spirit of Truth and the spirit of error" (I John 4:2).

An atheist who was once delivered, as the report goes, from an extremely serious situation, said: "Thank God." So likewise, any critic, examining the Scriptures, knows within himself that they were written by men speaking by the Eternal Spirit of Truth.

Chapter Nine

The Key Concept in the Thinking of the Apostle Paul

A term paper written by this author in a class in epistemology entitled "The Nature Of The Critical Argument" incorporated an idea put forth by Alfred J. Ayer. Ayer examined skepticism among other things and concluded that the question was "How Anything At All That Happened Was To Be Interpreted." Philosophy has been divided into different schools for a long time. In the early history of Greek philosophy there was speculative philosophy, the Idealist school of Socrates and Plato, the Empirical "Golden Mean" school of Aristotle and the Sophists who were Skeptical and pessimistic. Later, in modern times, the Empirical school and the Logical Positivist school among others appeared. These various schools have various outlooks on the world. They interpret various subjects in accordance with their views, which is quite natural. Theological and religious students and professors tend to use these philosophies consciously or unconsciously in interpreting religious matters.

While a list of "issues" considered in the treatment of Pauline thought could be made and the various interpretations analyzed and set forth and expounded upon, such as Paul's chronology in his work considered with respect to the Book of Acts and the Pauline epistles, or the influence of the

Greeks and Hebrews in Paul's eschatology, or any of the other issues, yet it is possible to set view against view and conclude that Paul was inconsistent, or unfair to the Jews, or quite different from the rest of the Apostles.

However, if one views Paul's thoughts in terms of Paul's conversion experience and his determination to know nothing except Christ and Him crucified, everything unfolds understandably. The conflicts that humans experience, the antitheses with respect to the Old Testament and the New Testament, Jew and Gentile, wise and unwise, bond and free, past and present, present and future, things above the earth and things on the earth, things on the earth and things below the earth, flesh and spirit, life and death, are all resolved in "Christ and Him crucified." It pleased God to gather all the negative things together in Christ that He might take them to the cross and then gather all positive things together in Him with the final result that God might be all in all. If this purpose of God is not seen or not sympathized with, a critic can never really understand Paul's thought because Paul had the mind of Christ. Therefore not a multidialectical quarrel is presented here but an effort to see things from Paul's point of view. "For I determined not to know anything among you, save Jesus Christ and him crucified" (I Cor. 2:2).

The cross had for a long time been used for execution. The Syrian rulers after the time of Alexander the Great used it, and even one of the Jewish rulers immediately near the time of the Maccabees used it. The Romans certainly used it. It was used to punish, often unjustly.

The Old Testament Prophets had prophesied about the crucifixion of the Messiah. Psalm 22 says: "All they that see me laugh me to scorn: they shoot out the lip, they shake the head, saying, He trusted on the Lord that He would deliver him: let Him deliver him, seeing He delighted in him" (7, 8). "For dogs have compassed me: the assembly of the wicked have inclosed me: they pierced my hands and my feet" (16). Isaiah 53 speaks greatly in detail of this. However, since the Jews went into captivity and later suffered under the

Seleucides and still later under the Romans, they looked for the Messiah to deliver them physically.

Pseudepigraphic literature often wrote of deliverance by angels and the success of the Maccabean revolt in great measure helped to condition Jewish thinking. Even before Christ the Essenes planned for the day when all the Goyim would be smitten. Thus it was difficult to conceive of the cross as a means of deliverance in any way. But God had written in the Book of the Prophet Daniel that the ancient world would be done away with by the Stone cut out of the mountain without hands. Messiah would be cut off "but not for Himself."

Therefore Paul was in darkness like most other people when Christ was crucified. His Pharisaic training depended upon a legal system of a prescriptive nature. Obedience achieved merit not only for this world but also for the next. Paul could not help but have misgivings, but he did not pursue them far, for he had another strong influence in his life, Hellenization. The Greek world treated aspects of human nature in stories of "gods." Guilt was inevitable because it was "fated." Later the ideas of the "gods" guarding law and order, although being themselves capricious, proceeded to approach the idea of natural processes and natural laws. Much of this, however, was due to the thinking of philosophers. By the time of Paul a somewhat syncretistic philosophy composed of the thinking of Socrates, Plato, Aristotle, and the Sophists was embodied in Stoicism. Wisdom was the main goal, and politics was considered to be the most important field of its application. While Greek thinking held life to be the sentence, by reincarnation, for past wrong, death was thought of as a liberation. Being crucified could "liberate" a person but it was hardly the way a noble-thinking Greek would choose. Death in connection with ruling and fighting was considered the most noble. It is true the "Mystery" religions offered mystical death in order that the devotee might become "one" with the "god," but the "mystical" dare not be real, that is, the death dare not be real. Therefore, for all practical purposes, crucifixion served only to discourage and punish crime.

So from neither Paul's Jewish background nor from his Greek background did worth attach itself to the cross. For him, before conversion, the cross of Christ was a part of shame, disobedience, myths, and lies. Fanatics should be dealt with as sternly as possible to restore order, he no doubt thought.

But when Jesus appeared to Paul on the Damascus road, all was changed. The meaning of the Passover Lamb became clear. The purpose of God, foretold in the Prophets, became clear. Paul was partly smitten because he realized that he had been in error and partly because he was set straight, but mostly because he saw the risen Christ, Lord of Israel and conqueror of death. He himself partook of Christ's death and resurrection in conversion but also when he was stoned. In terms of the Old Testament the weakness of human nature to keep the Law was eliminated and a better sacrifice for sins had been given. Atonement had been the high point of the Levitical system, and a great atonement, a perfect atonement, had been given in Christ. The old Adam was crucified and a New Adam had come, restoring the image of God and paradise. Better than the restoration of the Kingdom as it had been under David and Solomon was the eternal Kingdom of God. Even a better Jerusalem, a heavenly Jerusalem, was given. Fear had been the compelling force in the Jewish as well as the Hellenistic world. Now love was the great compelling power.

In Christ crucified, all of the sins of all people for all time had been dealth with. All things both in heaven and in earth had been gathered together in Christ. The divided self, divided thought, divided allegiance, divided love, and divided goal was all gone. The middle partition between bond and free, male and female, rich and poor, Jew and Greek, quick and dead, was gone (as well as wise and unwise).

Paul was free from the domain of sin. He could crucify unwanted desires and keep his body under control. He could crucify self when it prevented him from loving his neighbor as himself or even an enemy. He mortified the flesh by the spirit always bearing about in his body the dying of the Lord Jesus

71

Christ in order that the Life of Jesus might appear also. Sin and hate could never rest unless they killed. Thus as he came in contact with them he could crucify himself and sin with himself and in others in "filling up" the sufferings of Christ (Col. 1:24).

In a brief look at human problems in general, every relationship, whether it be between man and God, man and man (as neighbor), man and man (as enemy), past sin, present sin or future sin, past glory longed for, present glory longed for, or future glory longed for, all these were perfected by the cross, taking away the negative and giving the positive, as we continue in Christ.

As Paul met problems as a Christian and a missionary, these were dealt with in terms of Christ and Him crucified. Paul could listen to the Truth presented by the council at Jerusalem. He could carry the news of an easy yoke to the Gentiles, paid for at Calvary. He could practice what he preached and rejoice in enjoying salvation himself as he was used to save others. He was delivered from the condemnation that fell upon the Pharisees. "They say but do not." The impossible gulf between saying and doing had been breached. When he was stoned he knew Christ and Him crucified, but also "The power of His resurrection." He could rebuke a beloved brother speaking in the Truth. Having the Holy Spirit which Calvary made possible he could heal people, blind Bar-Jesus on Cyprus for a season, receive messages from Christ Himself, be used as an earthen vessel for Christ to speak through, admonish others to imitate him as he imitated Christ, face physical dangers, dangers of false brethren, false doctrine, false Apostles.

In dealing with cricumcision, idols and idol meat, fornication, the works of the flesh, the Lord's Supper, marriage, apostasy, or the Parousia he always could urge crucifixion of selfish desires and walking in the Spirit in Love, all made possible by Christ and Him crucified.

He and every Christian could partake of the benefits of Christ's death at Calvary, experience them daily in his body and soul, and work to grow up into the "fulness of the stature of Christ." Was there a problem of eating? "They are the enemies of the Cross of Christ." Was there a problem of fornication? "Put to death your members that are upon the earth." Did the people at Lystra want to worship him as a god? It was by the power of the crucified and risen Christ that the miracle had been wrought. Was there a problem of failing brethren? "Ye who are spiritual—spiritual because you are living the crucified life—restore such an one." The last enemy—death—would be destroyed and the whole creation be delivered. Nothing (Romans 8, principalities, powers, angels, life, death, height, depth, no creature) could or can separate us from the love of God which is in Christ Jesus.

Entrance into the church and into Christ were and are secured by faith and baptism which reenacts, effects, and partakes of "Christ and Him crucified." The Body of Christ is brought into fellowship repeatedly in the observance of the Lord's Supper. The inward man is renewed daily as Christians know Christ and Him crucified and, of necessity, partake of His resurrection. "For it was impossible for Him to be holden of them (the bonds of death)."

As the Crucified, Risen Saviour, Christ intercedes in heaven for Christians. The Holy Spirit, made possible by the death and resurrection of Christ, intercedes in prayer for Christians. The Christian always has an example of sufferings and a hope of deliverance, a motivation for work and love, a participation in eternal life and the Love of God which surpasses knowledge, all because of Christ and Him crucified. The rudiments of the world, the lust of the flesh, the lust of the eye and the pride of life, are all dealt with in "Christ and Him crucified."

Paul carried out his mission, living the crucified life, motivated by the Love of God, pressing on toward the mark of the prize of the high calling of God in Christ Jesus.

Even when every thought has been expended, the Christian knows the love of God which surpasses knowledge. Valleys are filled and mountains are leveled, the crooked is made straight and the rough is made smooth. The best is always yet to come for the Christian, all because of Christ and Him crucified. His blood always atones for sin and He always lives after the power of an endless life to give Christians life. The world required deceit, a coercing power, a system. God gives Truth, Life and Love now and forevermore because of "Christ and Him crucified." For the unconverted person or student the good news is that God so loved you that He gave His only begotten Son Jesus to be crucified for you and to bring you to Himself.

Conclusion and Invitation

When it is seen that the critical arguments against God and the Bible are equaled or even bettered, the way is open for a person to consider what the Bible itself says and to realize that there is hope for the hopeless and strengthtening for the believer. Why not accept Jesus Christ as your Lord and Saviour? No one has more to offer and you have nothing to lose. For everything you give up to accept Jesus, He will give you something better. He is the one person who paid the debt for sin with His sinless blood. Don't you want Him now and forever? All you have to do is to believe in Him, repent of your sins, accept Him as Lord and Saviour, confess Him as Lord and Saviour and be baptized. You will receive the remission of sins, the New Birth and the gift of the Holy Spirit.

For all the work presented in this book I give praise to God and thanks to the Lord Jesus Christ.

Appendix

The Role of Reason in Christian Ethics

In considering the "role" of reason and why it occupies the place it does in Christian ethics, it may be proper to make some reflections on reason itself. Some seem to identify it with the Logos ("The Light that lighteth every man that cometh into the world," Gospel of John, 1:9). Many have held it to be "Divine Reason." Immanuel Kant distinguished between "practical" reason and "pure" reason. Reason can be held in a mind that is conditioned by negative experiences ("even their mind and conscience is defiled," Titus 1:15) so that it is not allowed to operate properly. The Ancient Greeks "reasoned" many things from geometry to religion. There were the "classical," "skeptical," and "mediate" positions or points of view in which each went through some form of "reasoning."

The Leibnitz-Wolff philosophy had taken reason as a standard based upon the principles of "noncontradiction" and "sufficient" reason. Reason is able to take two (or more) ideas, principles, or objects and compare them, seeking likenesses and differences and mixed relationships between them. The revived Sophistical method of the ancient Greeks was used in the Middle Ages to attack "universals" and "forms" and was the base of the Skeptical method that attacked biblical doctrines in the Renaissance and even the Bible itself later. René Descartes used the method of doubt to arrive at the "indubital" of being (for he had asked, "how do I know I exist" when the skeptical method had questioned even existence itself) through the common denominator of "thinking." He said, in effect, "When I doubt my existence I think. When I am sure of it I think. In either case I think." *Cogito ergo sum*, that is, I think therefore I am. He used reason to make this deduction.

It remained, however, for Immanuel Kant to labor seriously with the nature of reason and to write his *Critique of Pure Reason*. The question had arisen as to whether or not a thing was known when it was not perceived (and even whether or not it existed when it was not perceived). David Hume had used the skeptical method and arrived at a place of denying causality, the cause and effect relationship. He held that the mind held perceptions in order by habit as a matter of association and not causality. He held that even the "self" was not an entity but a "bundle of perceptions."

Kant used Humes's book *An Enquiry Concerning the Human Understanding* as a reference to reflect upon the nature of reason and the mind. He thought it was possible to conceive of a transcendent object, but not to produce knowledge of it. The object was not perceived but conceived. It was a *"Ding An Sich,"* a "Thing in itself." He said that reason is limited to "phenomena" (events perceived by the senses) and could not know the "noumena" (things in themselves). He agreed that knowledge comes from empirical experience but held that the mind ordered the experiences according to categories (an unworthy comparison is perhaps seen in the "solid state circuits" of a television set). He considered the "A Priori" (things known, given, or existing innately apart from prior human experience) and the "empirical" factors (factors related to sense experience) and stated that there were four kinds of judgments that were possible. The first kind is the "analytical judgment" in which the predicate is contained in the subject and may be obtained by analysis of it. The second is the "synthetic" judgment in which the predicate is not contained in the subject. Then there is the "A Priori" judgment in which a universal and necessary connection is asserted between the subject and the predicate. Lastly, there is the "A Posteriori" judgment in which a universal and necessary connection between the subject and the predicate is not asserted.[1] (25 in Bibliography)

When the mind is required to agree with the object it perceives there is difficulty postulating universal truth. If, however, there is a shift so that the emphasis is not on an *object* perceived by a mind but rather a *mind* that perceives the object, the situation is changed:

> It will be seen that if this hypothesis is correct, all our experience begins with experience as Locke and the other empirics had insisted. But it does not necessarily follow, as they supposed, that it all arises from experience. Indeed, if Kant's hypothesis is correct, *all* knowledge, not just scientific knowledge, will contain elements which are not drawn from experience but are supplied by the mind itself. Such elements would be a priori in the sense demanded.[2] (25, in Bibliography)

This is criticized by W. T. Jones later in his book (being, it seems to me, involved in the same existential position that allowed the Sophists to move premises at will to form dilemmas and paradoxes or contradictions):

> According to Kant, in the rationalist argument given above, thought is taken in . . . two . . . totally different senses: in the major premise, as relating to an object in general and therefore to an object as it may be given in intuition; in the minor premise, only as it consists in relation to self-consciousness. In the latter sense, no object whatsoever is being thought; all that is being represented is simply the relation to self (as the form of thought).[3] (25, in Bib.)

Therefore, it seems that reason (considered by itself) in a

human mind has limitations (especially if a person is given to vice of one kind or another). But Reinhold Niebuhr says:

> Reason, insofar as it is able to survey the whole field of life, analyzes the various forces in their relationship to each other and, gauging their consequences in terms of the total welfare, it inevitably places the stamp of its approval upon those impulses which affirm life in its most inclusive terms.[4] (30, in Bib.)

This statement would seem to confirm the proposition that reason can be used as a tool or consulted as a guide. Now Kant was a Christian and had probably read the Bible. Scriptures like "Come, let us reason together, saith the Lord (Is. 1:18)," "Do unto others as you would have them do unto you" (paraphrase, Matt. 7:12), and "Speak every man Truth with his neighbor" (Eph. 4:25), would have been enough to start Kant thinking in terms of "other" and "all." For instance, the Golden Rule first stimulates the question, "What do I want others to do unto me?" and then "That is what I will do unto others." Thoughts will arise like: "If I have a need, and cannot supply it, I want others to supply it"; "If I am in a group I want the other person to treat me with the same esteem as I am willing to treat him"; etc. There is an implied standard of equality for two people and a universal for all people. So Kant could easily start from the Golden Rule and go on to arrive at a universal rule of equality, but could also ask, "What if everyone did it?"

Thus, using Scripture and reason, he could and did come to use reason in Christian ethics. His ethics were accepted by the Protestants because they offered ethics that were compatible with freedom of the individual but also with evangelism. His three axioms with respect to law and order and freedom have a force supplied by reason.

> The first is an axiom, i.e., an apodictically certain proposition which springs directly from the definition of external law (the harmony of the freedom of each with the

freedom of all others according to a universal law). The second is a postulate of external public law (the will of all united according to the principle of equality, without which no one would have any freedom). Third, there is the problem of how it is to be arranged that, in a society however large, harmony may be maintained in accordance with principles of freedom and equality (namely, by means of a representative system).[5] (16, in Bibliography)

Now he postulated duty for the sake of duty (or principle for the sake of principle) so that it could serve as an impartial rule and judge, if applied and accepted. R. Niebuhr said that reason, however, is prejudiced to the good men who postulate an unprejudiced rule for society. He also brought out the problem of applying individual ideals to a society. Because force is necessary in a society it is hard to use force in accord with the dictates of reason when not all men are reasonable and when situations are open to interpretation to men who have different interests.

However, if we reflect on the use of reason in Christian ethics, we see it to be extensive even if it is used to emphasize different things. Reason is used to systematize thoughts and language in terms of which questions are asked concerning the nature, possibility, validity, applicability, and effectiveness of ethics. These and other considerations are asked concerning the transendental element. Edward Long, Jr., in his book *A Survey of Christian Ethics* gives a good example of the use of reason as it analyzes ethics according to the deliberative, prescriptive, relational, and implementational motifs. If we look at the deliberative motif we can see that it is a set of procedures for arriving at the Christian norm, but also more than this. It is an attitude of mind that uses reason to inquire, reflect, pursue, discourse, deliberate, agree, disagree, classify, reshape, compare, systematize, survey, imply and relate among other things, the material, causes, ideas, and values and methods that will issue in the Christian norm.

Reason is used to formulate the rules of debating ethical

issues, the rules for weighing evidence, and the procedures for speculating about the future in general and any given ethic in particular. It seems to be true that the doctrine of Justification by Faith in Christianity can modify the ethical reflection as to the importance and extent of a norm and this is why, perhaps, that it has been stated that the use of reason in Christianity has varied. When reason has been used to form systematic theology it has in a related way formed a transcendent element for an ethic, for the justification of that ethic, and the base material for the interpretation of that ethic.

For instance, in Paul Tillich's theology of the corelation of culture and religion, in the consideration of these two in relationship to one another and to God, he said that they are both equidistant from God and went on to write the book *Love, Power and Justice.*

The Bible certainly says to "Prove all things, hold fast that which is good" (I Thess. 5:20). So even in the reflection of what constitutes proof, reason is used. Besides these things, if the Bible is taken as the basis of the norm for Christian ethics, it is certainly true that reason has been used in textual and historical criticism. We need not despair because criticism uses fallacious arguments and says "faith or reason," but realize that valid reasoning points to God and says: "faith *and* reason."[6]

Notes

1. W. T. Jones, *A History of Western Philosophy*, New York.

2. Ibid., p. 822.

3. Ibid., p. 839.

4. R. Niebuhr, *Moral Man in Immortal Society,* Charles Scribner's Sons Inc., N.Y., 1932, 1960, p. 27.

5. From *Critique of Pure Reason and Other Writings on Moral Philosophy* by Immanuel Kant, trans. Lewis White Beck, copyright 1949, Univ. Press, Reprinted by permission of the Bobbs-Merrill Company, Inc.

6. Selections from *Critique of Practical Reason and Other Writings on Moral Philosophy*, by Immanuel Kant, translated by Lewis White Beck, © 1949 by University of Chicago Press, reprinted by permission of the Bobbs-Merrill Company, Inc.

Final Notes

Sea shells were found high in a mountain. The skeletons of many different kinds of animals, normally separated, but which had crowded together because of some unusual condition, were found in a mountain cave. A think layer of water-laid clay was found, under which the intact remains of civilization were found in a number of places in the Mideast. (18 in Bibliography) "New" geologic formations were found under "old" geologic formations. Could not a great flood wherein "the fountains of the deep were broken up" (Gen. 7:11) have been the cause of these things?

Coal has been produced in a short time in a laboratory by the use of great heat and pressure. Thus there is no need to suppose that it took a long time to form the coal that is found in coal mines. An even more remarkable instance is reported by those who explored the giant meteor crater not far from Flagstaff, Arizona. When the meteor, hot from its plunge through the air, hit the earth, the heat and pressure on the earth materials were great and diamonds were formed instantly. It was just a matter of great heat and pressure.

The picture of Johann Peterson, who is or was eight feet two inches tall and who played in the motion picture *Prehistoric Women,* can be seen on page 122 of the October 2 issue of *Life Magazine* for 1950. This shows that there could have been giants like those mentioned in the Bible (Gen. 6:4 and I Sam. 17:4) and that it does not take a long time for biologic changes to take place.

One of the things criticized in the John Thomas Scopes evolution trial in Tennessee in 1923 was the miracle reported in the Bible wherein Joshua commanded the sun and moon to stand still for a day (Jos. 10:12-13). Modern astronomers have found a day missing in the calculations involving the sun, but in 1923 it was mentioned that the earth goes around the sun and it would have been the earth, not the sun, that stopped. Also that if the earth stopped people and buildings would be thrown through the air. This is because of the force of a moving body known as the "moment of inertia." It is equal to the mathematical product of the mass of the moving body times its velocity (Moment = Mass × Velocity). Now recent research has concluded that the "moment" is not just mechanical but involes electrical forces and the moment may be mostly (or entirely) "force fields." Now if God turned one-half of the force fields against the other half to balance them out to zero, the moment could have been zero, and produced the conditions of the miracle without having thrown people and buildings through the air. The electrical force on small rain drops is discharged as lightning when the small drops combine to form large rain drops. When a piece of paper is placed on top of water in a glass and a needle is placed on the paper, the paper becomes wet and can be pushed down away from the needle leaving it floating on the water suspended by static electrical forces. This is natural. But Jesus and Peter walked on the water (Matt. 14:25-29), and an angel freed Peter from prison by making his chains fall off and an iron gate open without being touched (Acts 12:10). This is supernatural. God created the natural forces, and there is no big gap between the natural and the supernatural for the believer. Jesus said a person can move mountains by faith, and it has been reported that scientists have witnessed a person bend a metal object with "mind power." At any rate, thousands of people witnessed the miracle of Fatima in France in 1917 wherein the sun became brighter and apparently came nearer the earth and wet ground and people were dried out in a few minutes (or moments), and many people were healed.

God gave men the powers of will and choice. If a person wills to do God's will and chooses to do God's will he can partake of the greatest miracle of all, the "New Birth." While God's work is witnessed in nature He has given His greatest witness and revelation in His Son the Lord Jesus Christ. "He hath revealed Him" (John 1:18). Accept Him, the better Life, and a happy eternal Life.

Bibliography

1. Ayer, A. J., *The Problem of Knowledge*, Penguin Books, Baltimore Maryland, 1956.
2. Barnett, Lincoln, *The Universe and Doctor Einstein*, Mentor Books as part of New American Library, Harper & Bros., New York, 1948.
3. Bently, John Edward, *Philosophy, An Outline History*, in New Students Outline Series, Littlefield, Adams & Co., Paterson, N.J., 1962.
4. Browne, E. H. & Ellicott, D. J., *The Inspiration of Scripture*, New York, T. Whittaker (2, Bible House) 1879.
5. Burch, Jack, *An Introduction to Galatians*, A Class Paper For Religion 607, Pepperdine University, L.A., Ca., Winter, 1973.
6. Bush, Dr. Vandevar, *Faith and Reason*, in *Fortune Magazine*, May, 1965.
7. Carnell, E. J., *An Introduction to Christian Apologetics*, Wm. B. Eerdmans Pub. Co., Grand Rapids, Michigan, 1948.
8. Dana, H. E., *New Testament Criticism*, The World Company, Inc., Publishers, Fort Worth, Texas, 1924.
9. Davidson, John, *Discourses on Prophecy*, John Henry and James Parker, London.
10. Davis, W. H., *Philosophy of Religion*, in *The Way of Life Series*, Biblical Research Press, Abilene, Texas, 1969.
11. Davis, W. H., *Science and Christian Faith*, in *The Way of Life Series*, Biblical Research Press, Abilene, Texas, 1968.
12. Ferguson, *The Authority of the Bible*, in *Abilene Christian*

Lectures, probably in *The Restoration Quarterly*, but available in a folder on reserve in the Pepperdine Library. L.A. Ca.

13. Gaussen, L., *Theopneusia, The Bible, Its Origin and Inspiration,* Hitchcok & Walden, Cincinnati; Nelson & Philips, New York.

14. Gibson, J. M., *The Inspiration and Authority of the Holy Scripture*, Fleming H. Revell Co., New York, Chicago, Toronto, London, Edinburg, 1912.

15. Grebe, John H., *Science Is Now Proving the Genesis Creation Account Is Correct,* in the July quarterly issue, 1964, *The Creation Research Society*, 4080 Gedden Road, Ann Arbor, Mich.

16. Gustafson, James M. & Laney, James T., Editor; Marty, Martin, H., General Editor, *On Being Responsible*, Harper Forum Books, Harper and Row, New York, 1968.

17. Guthrie, Donald, *New Testament Introduction*, Inter-Varsity Press, Box F, Downers Grove, Illinois, 1965.

18. Halley, H. Y., *Bible Handbook*, Zondervan Pub. House, Grand Rapids, Michigan, 1927.

19. Hastings, James, ed. (Selbie, John A. & Lambert, John C., Assistants, Article *"Inspiration"* in *A Dictionary of Christ and the Gospels.*, Charles Scribner's, New York (T. & T. Clark, Edinburg), 1906.

20. Holy Bible, The: King James Version.

21. Horn, Siegfried H., *Twenty-Five Years of Biblical Archeology in Review, Advent Review and Sabbath Herald*, Review and Herald Publishing Association, Washington, D.C., July 19, 1973.

22. Hoyle, Fred, & Narliker, Jayvant., Article on Cosmosology, *Science Section, Time Magazine*, July 1964.

23. Houston, Mike, *An Introduction to the Book of Romans,* Class Paper in Religion 607, Pepperdine University, Jan. 29, 1973.

24. Illingworth, J. R., *Reason and Revelation, An Essay in Christian Apology;* Macmillan & Co., Ltd., St. Martin St., London, 1908.

25. Jones, W. T., *A History of Western Philosophy,* Harcourt,

Brace and Company, New York, 1952.

26. Jowett, B. A., Trans., *Euthyphro* in Plato's *Republic*, A Vintage Book; Random House Publ., New York.

27. Kemeny, John, *A Philosopher Looks at Science*, D. Van Nostrand Co., Inc., New York, 1959.

28. Manly, Basil, *The Bible Doctrine of Inspiration*, A. C. Armstrong and Son, 714 Broadway, New York, 1927.

29. Metzger, Bruce H., *Patristic Evidence and the Textual Criticism of the New Testament*, in *New Testament Studies*, Vol. 18, 1872. Used by permission.

30. Niebuhr, Reinhold, *Moral Man in Immoral Society*, Charles Scribner's Sons, New York, New York, 1932, 1960.

31. Pache, René, *The Inspiration and Authority of Scripture*, Trans. by Helen I. Needham, Moody Press, Chicago, 1969. Used by permission.

32. Rimmer, Harry, *Internal Evidence of Inspiration* (John L. Frost Memorial Library Vol. 3), Wm. B. Eerdmans Pub. Co., Grand Rapids, Michigan, 1938.

33. Searles, Herbert L., *Logic and Scientific Method*, The Ronald Press Co., New York, 1956.

34. Skates, David, *An Introduction to the Gospel of John*, A Class Paper For Religion 607, G. Pepperdine University, Jan. 29, 1973.

35. Taylor, A. E., *Plato, the Man and His Work*, Meridian Books, Inc., New York, 1956.

36. Torrey, R. A., *Is the Bible the Inerrant Word of God?*, George H. Doran Co., 1922.

37. Wierman, Michael, *Luke—Acts, An Introduction*, A Class Paper for Religion 607, George Pepperdine University, Jan. 22, 1973.

38. Weber, Max, *Science as a Vocation*, Printed as *From Max Weber: Essays in Sociology*, edited and translated by H. H. Gerth and C. W. Mills, Copyright 1946 by Oxford University Press, N.Y., and reprinted and quoted in *Sociological Analysis* by Wilson and Kolb; Harcourt, Brace & Co., New York, 1949.

Appeal

If you are a Christian and this book has helped your faith by showing the working of fallacy in criticizing God and the Bible so that the criticisms are matched and the Bible can speak out freely, giving salvation and blessings, won't you help make it possible for other Christians to get this book also? You might even help a non-Christian become a Christian or a person who is on the verge of despair and suicide. The material in this book draws upon an education secured at the price of much effort and over $20,000, of course with the help of God and the Lord Jesus Christ. Won't you tell others about this book?

Sincerely,
Jack LeRoy Lease